ROBERT ICKE

Robert Icke is an award-winning writer and director, working in theatre and on screen. His recent production of *Player Kings*, starring Ian McKellen, opened at the Noël Coward Theatre before a national tour. His other recent work includes *Judas*, *Children of Nora* and *Oedipus* at Internationaal Theater Amsterdam, where until 2023 he was the inaugural Ibsen Artist in Residence. His adaptation of *Animal Farm* played an extensive national tour in 2022 and is slated for a London transfer. His monologue condensation of *Enemy of the People* starred Ann Dowd at Park Avenue Armory and was one of the first new pieces of theatre to play in New York post the pandemic shutdown.

In six years at the Almeida, he made eight productions; five transferred to the West End, and four to New York. These included his adaptations of *The Wild Duck*, *Mary Stuart* (also West End and National tour), *Uncle Vanya*, *Oresteia* (also West End; Schauspiel Stuttgart; Park Avenue Armory) and *1984* (co-created with Duncan Macmillan, also Broadway; West End; national and international tours). As a director, his productions included *Hamlet* starring Andrew Scott (also West End; Park Avenue Armory; and broadcast on BBC2), *The Fever* and *Mr Burns*. His play *The Doctor*, which played successful runs at Park Avenue Armory in 2023 and in the West End in 2022, remains in repertoire at both the Burgtheater in Vienna and Internationaal Theater Amsterdam, as well as in numerous new productions across the globe.

His awards include two Evening Standard Best Director Awards; the Critics' Circle Award, the Kurt Hübner Award (for his debut production in Germany); and the Olivier Award for Best Director, of which he was the youngest ever winner. He is a Fellow of the Royal Society of Literature.

Robert Icke

OEDIPUS

(long) after
Sophocles

NICK HERN BOOKS
London
www.nickhernbooks.co.uk

A Nick Hern Book

This version of *Oedipus* first published in Great Britain as a paperback original in 2024 by Nick Hern Books Limited, The Glasshouse, 49a Goldhawk Road, London W12 8QP

Reprinted in this revised edition in 2024

This version of *Oedipus* copyright © 2024 Robert Icke
Introduction copyright © 2024 Robert Icke
Afterword copyright © 2024 Professor Simon Goldhill

Robert Icke has asserted his moral right to be identified as the author of this version

Cover design by Nick Hern Books, from a design concept by James Illman

Designed and typeset by Nick Hern Books, London
Printed in the UK by Mimeo Ltd, Huntingdon, Cambridgeshire PE29 6XX

A CIP catalogue record for this book is available from the British Library

ISBN 978 1 83904 359 8

CAUTION All rights whatsoever in this play are strictly reserved. Requests to reproduce the text in whole or in part should be addressed to the publisher.

Amateur Performing Rights Applications for performance, including readings and excerpts, by amateurs in English should be addressed to the Performing Rights Manager, Nick Hern Books, The Glasshouse, 49a Goldhawk Road, London W12 8QP, *tel* +44 (0)20 8749 4953, *email* rights@nickhernbooks.co.uk, except as follows:

Australia: ORiGiN Theatrical, *email* enquiries@originmusic.com.au, *web* www.origintheatrical.com.au

New Zealand: Play Bureau, 20 Rua Street, Mangapapa, Gisborne, 4010, *tel* +64 21 258 3998, email info@playbureau.com

United States of America and Canada: Casarotto Ramsay and Associates Ltd, see details below

Professional Performing Rights Applications for performance by professionals in any medium and in any language throughout the world (including by amateur stock companies in the USA and Canada) should be addressed to Casarotto Ramsay and Associates Ltd, *email* rights@casarotto.co.uk, www.casarotto.co.uk

No performance of any kind may be given unless a licence has been obtained. Applications should be made before rehearsals begin. Publication of this play does not necessarily indicate its availability for performance.

www.nickhernbooks.co.uk/environmental-policy

INTRODUCTION

Does it matter that we know how it ends? The audience for *Medea*, then or now, will likely know as they take their seats that Medea will kill her children before the performance is over. Orestes, famous for killing his mother, does indeed kill his mother in the middle of the trilogy, *Oresteia*, that bears his name. Oedipus was famous for killing his father and marrying his mother. But neither thing actually happens in the play. It's all already happened.

Oedipus was famous (to Sophocles' audience) from Homer – who, in the *Odyssey*, has Odysseus visit the Underworld. There he meets Oedipus' mother, who admits having unknowingly married her son, after he had killed his father. Her name? Epikaste.

The tradition of Greek tragedy was to take a known story and re-tell it, changing it, re-making it to meet the present moment. Sophocles was to Homer as Shakespeare was to his sources: an audacious adaptor.

We can see this from two choices he makes: two single words. First: he changes Epikaste's name. Readers of Homer would expect Epikaste's arrival as a character: after all, she's Oedipus' mother, and they know what Oedipus needs to do with his mother before the play can end. That Sophocles' Oedipus begins the play married to Jocasta and not Epikaste (Medea begins her play with still-living children) is a clever misdirection. It has, they will come to learn, all already happened.

Second: Sophocles' *Oidipous Tyrannus*, when it was first performed in around 429 BCE, was part of a trilogy (the other two plays do not survive) that took second prize in the competition in which it premiered. It's traditionally become referred to as *Oedipus Rex*, which isn't quite accurate: Sophocles' title is Oedipus the Tyrant (not 'the King'). But that word has aged into a different meaning. Then, 'tyrant' was an enviable status, not a pejorative one: a leader 'chosen by acclaim', often one who served the social and economic cause of the ordinary people, rather than the aristocracy. So we might think of Sophocles' title not as 'Evil

Tyrant Oedipus', nor even as 'King Oedipus', but as 'Oedipus: the Chosen One'. The sharpness of its ambivalent irony is typical.

My election-night setting is an adaptation of that title, as well as a way to preserve the real-time, pressure-cooker unities (of time, place and action). Aristotle used Sophocles' play as the exemplary tragedy – and it really is a masterpiece: the backwards-forwards structure, the information reveal, the recurrence of threes (even the crossroads!), the way the weight of the dramatic irony never crushes the dramatic tension. Its emotion. And its terrible reminder that we don't know what we don't know.

I could go on about Sophocles' play or about how a 'hamartia' isn't a 'tragic flaw' or a moral failing, but simply a mis-step. But instead, a third word. Our word 'tragedy' is from theirs, 'tragōidia', meaning literally 'song of a goat' (a 'tragos' is a goat). We don't know exactly why. Some have argued a goat was the prize that the winning trilogy won, others that it relates to Dionysus (god of drama) who was associated with goats. I've come to prefer a third explanation. Goats were sacrificial animals, valuable possessions slaughtered as an offering to a deity: take this goat and grant me my prayer. The goat suffers so you don't have to: a scape-goat, who dies so good things can happen.

To work on the plays from this period is to bear witness to the extraordinary things they demand – and draw – from actors. And, as an audience gathers round the story of Oedipus and Jocasta, they perform a ritual that is nearly 2,500 years old, and one that in its structure echoes a sacrifice. Only now the goat *sings*: the actor suffers, lives the horror live in front of you, lives it so you experience it without it happening in your life. You stand distant from the suffering, but you bear witness; you feel something but you don't lose yourself.

Or at least, if you do, at the end, you are re-found. Life resumes again, after the theatre. Outside the play is the real space of safety, of free choice, of second chances; now the play has ended, life's time resumes again. What will we ask of ourselves? How might this evening's existential immunisation protect us, if the day should come when our life, like Oedipus', suddenly crumbles under our feet?

Robert Icke
September 2024

ACKNOWLEDGEMENTS

First, to the acting companies, in Amsterdam in 2018 and in London in 2024, whose input, at the first and last, is always invaluable. Then, in no particular order, to everyone who gave notes and thoughts and time and answers to questions: Ivo van Hove, Wouter van Ransbeek, Johan Reyniers, Denise Syndercombe-Court, Joe Winters, Luke Thompson, Lydia Wilson, Paul Rhys, Angus Wright, Stephen Grosz, Simon Goldhill, Helen Lewis, Emily Vaughan-Barratt, Ilinca Radulian, Joshua Higgott, Duncan Macmillan, Daniël 't Hoen, Sonia Friedman, Lizzie Manwaring, Alice Wordsworth, Rachel Taylor, Helena Clark, Heidi Lennard – and Zara Tempest-Walters. And to Peter Brook, whose wisdom and guidance one evening in Amsterdam in 2018 was genuinely inspiring – and remains so still.

This version of *Oedipus* was first performed in Dutch at the Internationaal Theater Amsterdam on 8 April 2018.

The cast was as follows:

LICHAS	Violet Braeckman
ANTIGONE	Hélène Devos
CORIN	Fred Goessens
CREON	Aus Greidanus Jr.
JOCASTA	Marieke Heebink
OEDIPUS	Hans Kesting
TEIRESIAS	Hugo Koolschijn
MEROPE	Frieda Pittoors
POLYNEICES	Harm Duco Schut
DRIVER	Bart Slegers
ETEOCLES	Josha Stradowski
Writer/Director	Robert Icke
Set	Hildegard Bechtler
Costume	Wojciech Dziedzic
Lighting	Natasha Chivers
Sound	Tom Gibbons
Video	Tal Yarden
Translation	Rob Klinkenberg
Assistant Director	Daniël 't Hoen

This version of *Oedipus* was first performed in English at Wyndham's Theatre, London, on 15 October 2024 (previews from 4 October), produced by Sonia Friedman Productions.

The cast was as follows:

TEIRESIAS	Samuel Brewer
CREON	Michael Gould
LICHAS	Sara Hazemi
JOCASTA	Lesley Manville
DRIVER	Gary McDonald
CORIN	Bhasker Patel
ANTIGONE	Phia Saban
ETEOCLES	Jordan Scowen
OEDIPUS	Mark Strong
MEROPE	June Watson
POLYNEICES	James Wilbraham

Understudies
Jim Creighton
Derek Elroy
Sara Hazemi
Celia Nelson
Jake Rory

Writer/Director	Robert Icke
Set	Hildegard Bechtler
Costume	Wojciech Dziedzic
Lighting	Natasha Chivers
Sound	Tom Gibbons
Video	Tal Yarden
Casting	Julia Horan CDG
Associate Directors	Lizzie Manwaring
	Alice Wordsworth
Company Stage Manager	Heidi Lennard
Deputy Stage Manager	Natalie Braid
Assistant Stage Managers	Ben Dootson
	Louise Quartermain

A NOTE ON THE TEXT

A forward slash (/) marks the point of interruption of overlapping dialogue.

A comma on a separate line (,) indicates a pause, a rest, a silence, an upbeat or a lift. Length and intensity are context dependent.

Square brackets [like this] indicate words that are part of the intention of the line but are *not* spoken aloud.

Two speakers followed by (*chorus*) indicates the two lines are to be spoken simultaneously.

The stage directions here are presented for ease of reading, not as a thorough account of the production decisions.

Future productions are welcome to make other decisions, and encouraged to adjust characters' ages and key dates (i.e. Laius' death, Oedipus' and Jocasta's wedding, and so on) to suit their needs; though the age gap between Oedipus and Jocasta should remain thirteen years.

When [TIME] appears, the characters should refer in real-time to the live 'election result' countdown clock. If not using such a clock, an approximate time until the result is due (e.g. 'twenty minutes') will be fine.

This text should be played without an interval.

CHARACTERS

OEDIPUS
CREON
MEROPE
JOCASTA
ANTIGONE
CORIN
LICHAS
TEIRESIAS
POLYNEICES
ETEOCLES
DRIVER

This text went to press before the end of rehearsals and so may differ slightly from the play as performed.

It begins before

in the headquarters of a major political campaign: phones ring, printers spool out documents, screens flash graphs and faces and the endless news cycles tumble on to each other, it's alive, full of action, full of posters of OEDIPUS' *face, a 'days to go' digital counter shows that there are fifteen days to go –*

and then a curtain falls.

Projected onto it, OEDIPUS *on a screen, talking live to a huddle of reporters, the camera tight on his face, maybe microphones, etc., in shot. He's speaking impromptu, no notes, he's midway through:*

OEDIPUS   My children – my brothers and sisters – all of them. What will they inherit? What kind of start?

'Are you the country's father?'

    A father to the country? (*he laughs*) Perhaps the country needs a father after thirty years of coalition and compromise – we'll find out tonight.

'Do you think you're going to win?'

    The result will be with us in a couple of hours. I have always said that if I am offered the role, I will accept it. My team tell me it's looking good. But I say: count on nothing till you hold it in your hand.

'People are saying, you must be aware of this, that the symbolism of another white man…'

    Should there have been a different set of applicants? That's not my job to fix – at least, not yet. Now, let me ask you one: do you think this job is important enough that symbolism shouldn't be allowed to be a factor?

But you know what? This was a new movement, a tiny new movement, only three years ago. This didn't seem possible then – not least because I am the candidate that people wanted and not the one the people in the suits told them they should want. (I'm wearing a suit, I know.) My point is: things change fast.

'Any final thoughts on the country the polls say you'll be leading tomorrow?'

Final thoughts on the way things are? I think what everyone thinks. We're sick. The civic body is ill. And that isn't trees and chemicals in lakes – it's us – it's us – we're sick.

The water got poisoned – and we got used to the taste. And while we were sleeping, while we were staring into our palms, they deliberately dragged us back in time – backwards to a time when the rich were rich, and the poor were poor, backwards to when people who weren't like us deserved persecution, backwards until rumours and lies were the same as the truth – and we've seen that in this campaign.

My opponent loves the idea that this country isn't my country. He doesn't say I couldn't do the job – he says I'm not from here. My identity doesn't fit. It's nasty and it's stupid – and it's wrong. We're going to release my birth certificate later tonight but – what is underneath that idea that where we were born is of premium, unmatchable importance? Do we really believe that deep down inside each of us there's one single self, a hard centre formed at the moment of birth, and destined never to change? Does all the rest – does a

person's whole voyage through time – does
that mean nothing? But we'll release the birth
certificate, and there an end.

Flashbulbs intensify.

> And those who know the truth about my birth,
> and believe it, might still say 'he came from
> peasant stock' (and I did) 'he has no experience
> of political office' (and I don't!) 'and so his
> marriage must be [political] – he married her
> because she was married to Laius' – and yes,
> my wife was married to the previous holder of
> this office, you all knew her years before I did.
> But a marriage like ours isn't about politics.
>
> And yes, it's been thirty-four years since Laius'
> death. A lot of words have been written about
> that gap, the lack of a leader since then,
> the need for one – or not (!) – and endless
> rumours and theories about how he died.
> So. It may be that later tonight, I will stand
> before you as Laius' successor, the inheritor
> of his legacy. And if I am, I will open the
> investigation into his death and personally
> lead it myself, on public record.
>
> To lead a country is an act of creation. And
> what gets made? A world. A future.
>
> But do you hear that?
>
> ,
>
> The ice is breaking. Something shifting
> ground. They tell me there's a storm coming
> tonight. That sounds about right.
>
> I'll see you all in two hours. Thanks.

and the curtain rises.

The same room, now decisively abandoned. Pizza boxes, water bottles, discarded T-shirts, half-deflated balloons. It's not yet been a day but it has been left and left for the final time and is now halfway through being packed up. Throughout the evening, attendants pack more and more things into boxes, and carry them away, until, by the end, the room stands white and empty.

The 'days to go' countdown clock, big red electronic numbers, is counting down in days, weeks, minutes and seconds, to the moment the election result will be decided. Now it shows only an hour and fifty minutes, and the time flows away.

MEROPE, *an elderly, motherly woman, held-together, waits. She's wearing an outdoor coat. The interview we've just watched with* OEDIPUS *plays on a screen and she watches it, almost severely.*

People moving stuff and moving stuff and moving stuff.

OEDIPUS *enters with* CREON.

CREON It's like you don't even know you're doing it. You can ignore a question – you know, nothing bad happens if a question's left unanswered.

OEDIPUS *catches sight of* MEROPE *– stops –*

OEDIPUS Mum.

You look beautiful.

Hello.

MEROPE Hello

There's tension here, between these two – is it sexual? We might wonder.

OEDIPUS I didn't see you there.

MEROPE	No
OEDIPUS	I didn't / see you
MEROPE	I know.
OEDIPUS	I didn't know you were going to be here tonight –
MEROPE	I didn't tell you.

,

OEDIPUS	How is he?
MEROPE	The same.

,

OEDIPUS	I hadn't realised you were going to be here – I / didn't know
MEROPE	I need some time with you alone.

JOCASTA *comes in.*

OEDIPUS	Honey, my *mum* is here –
JOCASTA	Hello
OEDIPUS	look at this –
JOCASTA	How long have you been here?
MEROPE	An hour or so. This place is a tip.
JOCASTA	Why clean, is what I always say – you can't prevent decay – (*to* OEDIPUS) but the campaign is over and we have all earned a little celebration
OEDIPUS	I'm – a bit *stunned* by the fact that my mother has travelled all the way here to surprise me tonight, which must have been your [JOCASTA's] doing – a *little celebration* –

JOCASTA   She –

MEROPE   No, that isn't why I came. I didn't know.

,

This is slightly awkward – and we realise there is some tension between MEROPE *and* JOCASTA.

JOCASTA   *Well* – tonight is a night for us *all* to celebrate –

MEROPE   You know it's not his birthday.

JOCASTA   I do know that, yes –

OEDIPUS   Ladies –

CREON   Sorry – it's a very / busy

MEROPE   I need to talk to him

OEDIPUS *has seen* ANTIGONE, *his daughter, clutching a book – early for the 'surprise' reveal.* JOCASTA *annoyed that the plan for the evening hasn't been adhered to.*

ANTIGONE   Dad!

OEDIPUS   And the scholar returns!

JOCASTA   oh wonderful

OEDIPUS   Is the gang all here – ?

ANTIGONE   I'm here for the victory party

OEDIPUS   well you're two hours early

ANTIGONE   well I brought work

OEDIPUS   and what mystery of human nature are we unscrambling this evening?

ANTIGONE   The difference between a paradox and a riddle.

OEDIPUS   And they say academics have become irrelevant. What is it?

ANTIGONE	what?
OEDIPUS	The difference
ANTIGONE	One's got a solution – one's just something you have to live with?
OEDIPUS	Sounds like the choice on the ballot paper
JOCASTA	Oedipus
OEDIPUS	One has solutions. One you'd just have to live with.
JOCASTA	It's all behind us, the campaign's over, the polls are closed.
MEROPE	I need to speak to him
CREON	Sorry. Not now. He has a meeting.
OEDIPUS	Cancel it.
CREON	No.
JOCASTA	What is it?
CREON	It's me.
OEDIPUS	Now? We can speak later
CREON	After tonight, you have no later
OEDIPUS	One night off. One night off is all I ask
CREON	(*to* JOCASTA) Could you please tell your husband / that
OEDIPUS	(*to* JOCASTA) Could you please tell *your brother*
JOCASTA	Overruling, two against one, how long will it take?
CREON	[Thank you] – really not very long
OEDIPUS	I'm guessing we still have security here tonight?

CREON   No, because I have absolutely no idea how to do my job –

OEDIPUS   The tragedy is: you think that's a joke.

JOCASTA   It's a conversation, yes? Do it, have it, then we can relax –

    JOCASTA *exits, as she does, kissing* OEDIPUS –

MEROPE   Oedipus, I need a few minutes with you. Alone.

OEDIPUS   Why?

MEROPE   If it were for public consumption, it wouldn't need to be alone.

OEDIPUS   Okay. Well, hold fire – and later, we'll catch up. Corin, my friend, could you take my mother and look after her with the utmost care and attention?

    CORIN (*elderly, kindly*) *has been on stage – fussing, tidying – for a while.*

CORIN   It would be my pleasure

OEDIPUS   And before the evening is out, we will find a moment to talk.

MEROPE   Very good.

LICHAS   The third office is already cleared –

CORIN   I'll bring you to it – this way

    MEROPE *leaves with* CORIN – OEDIPUS *catches* LICHAS, *his personal aide, as she goes out.*

OEDIPUS   So, an unscheduled surprise?

LICHAS   It would be less surprising if we'd put it on the schedule.

OEDIPUS   You drew the shortest of short straws – being here tonight

LICHAS   I wanted to be. Honestly.

She follows them. OEDIPUS *looks at* CREON. OEDIPUS *changes his clothes.*

OEDIPUS   Now let me get ahead of you – and admit that I didn't say word for word what you / wanted me to say

CREON   It's Captain Exceptional again, the superhuman, saviour of the world –

OEDIPUS   You can't just put words in my mouth

CREON   That is literally what speechwriting is

OEDIPUS   I will speak from myself. I will say what I want to say as I accept the position for which I have spent a year running. With help. Yes. But it is me they are electing and me they will hear. I will speak from myself. All right?

CREON   Most leaders would discuss strategy *with their teams* before announcing it to the world. And *this* is complex. No plan. No discussion. The birth certificate – and God, reopening Laius' death?

OEDIPUS   If I say in public we're doing it, then we have to do it. It keeps you on your toes –

CREON   It should have been *discussed*. It's complex and, as usual, there's more involved than you realised / when you

OEDIPUS   I am so sick of it being a problem to this campaign that I am not dishonest –

CREON   Your image, the way you are *seen*, is something we have to control

OEDIPUS   Now? No. I am me. I am me. The campaign's done. It's over.

TEIRESIAS   Oedipus

A new voice. Both of them puzzled.

OEDIPUS   Who's this?

TEIRESIAS   Oedipus – I know your voice.

TEIRESIAS, *blind, appears, somehow already in the room.*

OEDIPUS   (*to* CREON) Did you get me a stripper?

CREON   I'm sorry, I think you've come to the wrong place

TEIRESIAS   Oedipus, you can hear me – you are *here*

CREON   How did you get in here?

TEIRESIAS   The child brought me.

OEDIPUS   Everyone welcome.

CREON   I do apologise: this is supposed to be a secure location, and you don't have permission to be / here

TEIRESIAS   *Oedipus –*

LICHAS   I'll get security

OEDIPUS   Oh come on, look at him – if he manages to assassinate me against those odds, fair play to him.

OEDIPUS, *kind, leads him, sits him down.*

                     Come. Can I have them get you a drink of / any sort?

TEIRESIAS   No. I don't want to make you angry –

OEDIPUS	I'm not angry – why would I be angry? But I'm afraid, my friend, I only have a few minutes, you've turned up on a pretty / busy night.
CREON	I *know* him. He's one of the… people. The future-telling people.
OEDIPUS	Is he? The ones who thought I'd lose.
TEIRESIAS	You will lose.

,

OEDIPUS	Happy to have you here. Well, you wanted us to meet them and now here we are meeting them. My gift to you.
CREON	People *listen* to them
OEDIPUS	*Some* people listen to them
CREON	*Hundreds of thousands of people worldwide* listen to them
TEIRESIAS	Oedipus –
OEDIPUS	(*to* CREON) Well I'm not seeking voters *worldwide* – and this is *late*: I mean, I'm up for going back through the fights you lost, but we're really facing the wrong way if we're doing this *once the polls have closed* –
CREON	if we'd brought them on side, they have an *audience*
OEDIPUS	Having an audience is easy. Hard part's having something to say.
	(*to* TEIRESIAS) Bad night for you if the polls tell the truth.
TEIRESIAS	The polls mean nothing. It will be Creon.

,

OEDIPUS   This is Oedipus. Creon's here too. But Creon isn't actually on the *ballot* for tonight's election

TEIRESIAS   I made no prediction about tonight's / election

OEDIPUS   You said it would / be Creon

TEIRESIAS   but not tonight.

    OEDIPUS *looks up.*

OEDIPUS   I didn't catch your name

TEIRESIAS   Oedipus –

    TEIRESIAS *is reaching for* OEDIPUS' *hand.*

              We are human, you and I

              nothing more. Nothing.

OEDIPUS   Yes –

              ,

TEIRESIAS   but a whole world lies under your feet.
                A whole universe, somewhere: *here*, unseen
                and tonight it slips free –

OEDIPUS   Yes (?)

TEIRESIAS   I came to warn you. Not to help you.
                Powerless to help you: to see the disease in the cell is not to know the cure.

OEDIPUS   [Enough.] If this is a joke, it's both funny and well-executed, but what we're going to do is this…

TEIRESIAS   There is nothing to be done – it is *over*.
                Over all of it, some other, some *other* truth is coming, was always coming, it is all over

OEDIPUS	What is all over? What disease?
TEIRESIAS	It starts with Laius – you are right to look a second time –
OEDIPUS	Laius' death, you mean?
TEIRESIAS	It was not as we were told –
CREON	Oedipus, could we speak for a / moment
OEDIPUS	Let him speak. Please – go on.
TEIRESIAS	I'm frightened.

TEIRESIAS *seems emotional.*

	I don't want to make you angry
OEDIPUS	I'm not going to be angry – please. I'm listening. Go on. Continue.
TEIRESIAS	The sky is so huge, so frighteningly huge, so pitilessly blank, indifferent, and the wide flights of the birds – the life of the human being is a tiny track mark on the earth, a helpless scratch – and what there is in store for you is *cruel*. Blood on the glass. Time turns, sets a backward course, starts for the start with *speed*: the fragile moments drop, unravelling, reversing, unwound, back to the beginning. My speech is out of time.
OEDIPUS	Sit down – sit *down*
TEIRESIAS	you don't understand – but I can't help you. I cannot help you. It's over.
CREON	Is something coming to us?
TEIRESIAS	The answer to that question is always yes.

CREON	Tonight?
TEIRESIAS	To speak further will only make him angry.
OEDIPUS	I'm not going to / be angry
TEIRESIAS	He finds the answers. He hunts them to the end. To understand the details will not change a thing. Get me *out – get me out – get me out –*
OEDIPUS	What happened to Laius? / What do you know?
CREON	Oedipus, please –
TEIRESIAS	To understand is to see it yourself
OEDIPUS	my God, the enigmas –
TEIRESIAS	These are not enigmas. That you fail to understand it does not make it an enigma. You will be forced to see who you are
OEDIPUS	I know / who I am!
TEIRESIAS	you do not know what you have done, you do not know who you *are*, and here now there is nothing to be done. I've said too much. I want to *leave* –
OEDIPUS	You realise that, once tonight is over, there will be other ways for me to persuade you to speak.
TEIRESIAS	It will be Creon.

OEDIPUS *starts to get angry now.*

OEDIPUS   My wife's brother *does not have his name on the ballot.* He literally *cannot* be *elected.* So whose idea was this? Surprise guest. Little confidence boost at the last moment, try and get inside my head. Was that it?

	I am trying to *change things*. I am trying to move us forwards.
TEIRESIAS	to break every boundary is to break *every* boundary. The one that holds havoc from control. The one holding human from animal.
OEDIPUS	It must be hard, I understand that, to accept that there's no money in new-age fear-mongering or fortune-teller cryptic crossword clues
	Why did you come? Why come at all?
TEIRESIAS	I came to / warn you
OEDIPUS	You came because you want to psych me out. Fear beats hope every time: blind in your soul as well as your eyes / it must be deeply humiliating, these days, to have to claim you can see the future
TEIRESIAS	Oedipus – I
TEIRESIAS	I came to warn you, Oedipus.
OEDIPUS	Then WARN ME. Come on. Let's go. Pre-dict. Three things you've seen that *actually* come true –
TEIRESIAS	Three [predictions]?
	Yes.
	One. You find the truth of Laius' death – that you yourself are the killer you seek.
OEDIPUS	Hilarious. And was I *sleeping* when I murdered Laius?
TEIRESIAS	you're sleeping now.
	Two. You bring the darkest shame on your parents – your father's killer – and your mother's lover.

OEDIPUS	Say that again
TEIRESIAS	I said you would / be angry
OEDIPUS	Are you surprised? Are you surprised I'm angry, when my father is lying in a hospital bed – are you surprised I'm angry when you dishonour my mother, I give you my valuable time, I allow you to spout your nonsense and you have the audacity – are you *surprised* I'm angry?
TEIRESIAS	I have never once experienced surprise.
OEDIPUS	Let's see if we can help with that –

OEDIPUS *throws* TEIRESIAS *onto the floor.*

CREON	(*chorus*) Oedipus
ANTIGONE	(*chorus*) Dad – he can't defend himself
OEDIPUS	He's a fraud. And the two of you have *decided*, for some poisonous reason – you [CREON] smuggled him in here *tonight, for one thing* –
CREON	*no*
TEIRESIAS	Three. You said three. The third is this:
	It turns everything around, but itself stands still.
OEDIPUS	'It turns everything around, but itself stands still.'
	And what the fuck is that supposed to mean?
TEIRESIAS	When you can answer that question – for the first time you will know yourself.
	,
OEDIPUS	Get him out, call security – let's see if they can find out who he is, let's not waste any more time.

CREON	Lichas! Corin!
OEDIPUS	Where's that child?
TEIRESIAS	You *see*. And you wish / you were blind.
OEDIPUS	stop talking.
	Thank you.
	(*to* CREON) I thought we'd put this in the past. The frustration at being second-in-command. I understood that. What I don't understand is –

LICHAS *comes in with security,* OEDIPUS *points at* TEIRESIAS:

> Him. Out. (*straight back to* CREON) I mean, it's a badly kept secret that you've got your own ambitions – but *that* was a joke – but you have been *on my side* with this stuff

TEIRESIAS	I did not predict he would win the / election – he knew *nothing* of what I know –
OEDIPUS	Goodbye –
TEIRESIAS	Creon did not know

OEDIPUS *bangs the table or something.*

OEDIPUS	*Goodbye.*

LICHAS *and security take* TEIRESIAS *out.*

CREON	I am / on your side. I didn't *know*
OEDIPUS	You want to attack me? Fine. But at least have the manners to cover it up. There's backstabbing and there's backstabbing but this is straightforward amateur hour –
ANTIGONE	Dad –

CREON   Oedipus – do you want to try and listen – you know, just to see what it feels like?

OEDIPUS   'It will be Creon', it makes no *sense* – it's not a strategy – though, presumably, you're already planning for next time around –

CREON   No. That's not what I want.

OEDIPUS   It's also not how it *works*. You're never going to be the chosen one – these things are done on *merit* now. Which is not an area in which you excel. Which is also not a secret.

ANTIGONE   Dad, leave him alone

CREON   You're insane. This is totally insane.

OEDIPUS   You want to know something else that isn't a secret? Your mediocrity. Your middle-of-the-road, play-to-the-crowd, behind-the-curve, little-boy-anxious way of not-quite-dealing with the hard questions, the big issues and the burning fucking problems of the time.

ANTIGONE   Stop it –

OEDIPUS   And your fear. The fact that you don't *dare* until the moment's gone past. Your fundamental commitment to inaction. Too busy checking the rules. And (!) here we are – when do you try and sabotage me? When does the assassin look lively with the knife? On the night I've already won the election. By definition: too late.

,

I might not like you, but I do know you.

CREON   Oedipus, I haven't done anything wrong. I didn't know he would be here. Or what he was going to say. I didn't ask him to say anything –

OEDIPUS   And you've never had any ambition to win an election?

CREON *opens his mouth to say 'no', and falters – that split second is all it needs –*

Exactly. *Exactly.*

CREON   For fuck's sake, I wanted you to win.

OEDIPUS   Past tense

CREON   Why would I bother with the hours of work, the campaign, the lack of sleep, fighting you when you've got it wrong – *like now*, paying you the compliment of reacting to your paranoid, arrogant bullshit, why would I have bothered – writing for you, thinking endlessly about what you should say, about the right course of action, obsessing over images and photo ops after photo ops of sheets of paper with your fucking face on them and literally putting extra hours in your day by ensuring we fly with the sun – and all just to try and make sure that you win. Why would I bother? I want you to win. I always wanted you to win. You're not even listening to me.

OEDIPUS   My instinct is shouting you down, I'm afraid. And I trust my instincts more than I trust / you.

CREON   So you're not going to listen to what has actually happened?

OEDIPUS   What has actually happened is this. You don't want me looking into the death of Laius, which –

LICHAS *enters, with a folded sheet of paper. The men fall silent.*

LICHAS   Sorry – are we ready?

She goes to CREON *with the paper, when:*

OEDIPUS	To me, please. Thanks.

He reads it. It's election info, but it's not important yet –

LICHAS	Do you want the updates directly as they come in?
OEDIPUS	I do. Is he out of the building?
LICHAS	Yes.
OEDIPUS	And the child?
LICHAS	I didn't see a child, but
OEDIPUS	So now we have an unaccounted-for child in the building. Thank you.

LICHAS *leaves. A pause.*

CREON	I had nothing to do with what he said. Nothing.
OEDIPUS	It's quite the story. I'm Laius' killer. The new one *murdered* the old one.
CREON	Fine. You'll find out tomorrow.
OEDIPUS	About what?
CREON	About Laius. And what you'll find out is the only thing I've done is try and protect you – which has been exactly the same, every single day, for the last three years of my life.
OEDIPUS	So you think all this is thanks to you?
	,
CREON	You think you have nothing to thank me for?
OEDIPUS	The occasional reminder of the rules aside –
CREON	Yeah, because it's not like understanding the rules of this election has helped us in any

	way, it's not like the specific wording of the relevant laws has been *beneficial* to the ways we've found to get / round them
OEDIPUS	After tonight, I won't be needing you.
CREON	You won't [be needing me?] –
	,
	Oedipus, take some time to think
OEDIPUS	I have. We're done. I'll tell your sister in the morning. I will *not* be under*mined* from with*in*.
CREON	Right. Well, then there's nothing I can / say.

But POLYNEICES *has run at* OEDIPUS *from behind, and put hands over his eyes, as quickly the others move through the space, pulling trolleys, assembling tables* –

OEDIPUS	I see nothing – only darkness, the darkness is –
	interrupted by the noise of cutlery and whispering which suggests to me that somehow my wife has organised a – surprise *meal* –

He's said this just as his eyes have been uncovered and the image is ready, everyone facing him – and no one knows quite what to do. He's solved the surprise before it surprised him.

	Well – go on then!
ALL	SURPRISE

ANTIGONE *takes a picture with a camera she has around her neck. His sons* ETEOCLES *and* POLYNEICES *are also in front of him.*

OEDIPUS	My boys ARE here! I haven't seen you all for – what? – three weeks?
ETEOCLES	Nine weeks, but it's fine –

JOCASTA	You couldn't play along and be surprised –
OEDIPUS	when you know, you know –
JOCASTA	You will be the death of me –
OEDIPUS	and where are the *dates*? no plus-ones?
POLYNEICES	(*fast*) no
ETEOCLES	tonight's not the night for meeting the parents, Dad
OEDIPUS	tonight might be your last chance, for a while –
	A NIGHT OFF!
	This is incredible

CREON *moves through the room, perhaps touches* ANTIGONE's *arm. He doesn't sulk but he also doesn't speak.* JOCASTA *catches* CREON, *on the quiet* –

JOCASTA	What's wrong? I can tell from your face –
CREON	It's him [OEDIPUS]. I'll tell you later.
OEDIPUS	No, it's him and I'll tell you later –
JOCASTA	He's angry about the investigation
OEDIPUS	How do you know that?
JOCASTA	I was with him as you made your unannounced announcement –
OEDIPUS	Honestly, marry your brother –
JOCASTA	You have always been jealous of my relationship with my brother
OEDIPUS	That is not even a little bit / true

JOCASTA   And given that we are, what? A couple of
                hours away now –

                OEDIPUS *knows that she can't see her watch without her
                glasses, which she isn't wearing – this between them is totally good-
                humoured, as* POLYNEICES *and* ETEOCLES *throw a ball
                to each other –*

OEDIPUS   Will you just accept that you need glasses and
                wear / them

JOCASTA   – given that, before the sun has gone all the
                way down and come all the way up, you are
                going to be running the *country my brother lives
                in*, given that he will be paying his *taxes* to you,
                maybe you can, just for a change, Let It Go

OEDIPUS   For you [I would do] anything – but /
                there's – NO –

                POLYNEICES *throws a ball at* OEDIPUS *and then runs.*
                OEDIPUS *chases* POLYNEICES *and* ETEOCLES –
                *wild, off around the set – crashing into things, chaotic – this can
                take some time.*

                *Meantime – chairs are assembled, an assortment from the office
                (*CORIN, JOCASTA, LICHAS *and* ANTIGONE *have
                transferred the food to the table).*

                Until full speed, OEDIPUS *comes flying round a corner and
                nearly crashes into* MEROPE *– who stands at the door, genuinely
                surprised.*

OEDIPUS   (*to* MEROPE) Mother

E/P/A   Nana!

OEDIPUS   you are fashionably late for the surprise –

MEROPE   I wasn't informed there would *be* a surprise –

JOCASTA   (*to* MEROPE) Help yourself to a seat –

OEDIPUS — I'm *happy* you're here

MEROPE — we still need to speak / Oedipus

OEDIPUS I know — the whole evening stretches ahead of us — there is *time time time time TIME* — I don't have to shake any hands or race in a guarded car to an overnight plane or rewrite a portion of another speech or learn the names of donors — I just have an evening and my mother and my *wife* and my sons and my daughter and

ETEOCLES — and absolute power.

OEDIPUS I don't have that yet, amigo. But I do have my favourite food. Is this your recipe, Mum?

JOCASTA It's my recipe

MEROPE Why are we having dinner *here*?

JOCASTA Your son was determined to spend tonight here

OEDIPUS I announced my candidacy here. All our best ideas happened here. It felt right that the old place got to see the final night, rather than some classical suite in a grand hotel —

MEROPE And where are all your staff?

OEDIPUS Preparing parties or measuring the walls above their desks or updating their résumés — boys, is this really what you two are wearing?

ETEOCLES *and* POLYNEICES *are not wearing suits.*

ETEOCLES We have suits but we are not going to put them on yet because we will only find some way of ruining them, because we always ruin everything

OEDIPUS   I hear the voice of the mother

JOCASTA   'The mother'? You *are not* one of the children. I actually tell people, I have four children, two at twenty, one at twenty-three and one at fifty-two –

ANTIGONE And one that died.

,

JOCASTA   Yes – I don't know what you think you're doing –

ANTIGONE It's called telling the truth –

JOCASTA   I know you know that that's private information, maybe you're trying to be morbid or just trying to upset / me, either way, you're achieving both – and tonight is the night for *neither*.

ANTIGONE So because it died, we forget it? I'll sit in the other room

JOCASTA   You'll sit right there. Tonight is not your night.

CORIN *has been serving the food with* LICHAS, *everyone is basically seated by now at their places. This meal scene should proceed quickly and with overlaps and ad libs and feel like a real family, really sitting down for dinner.*

OEDIPUS *eyes the food greedily.*

OEDIPUS   I have spent a year, a whole year, eating whatever local delicacy they put into my hand. I have eaten some things that go significantly beyond most people's definition of 'food'.

MEROPE   This room is huge –

CORIN   Even bigger before they put the walls in – all put in for the campaign – and they're being taken back out tonight. Not much of a dining room, I'm afraid –

OEDIPUS   It is improvised, thrown together, spontaneous, much like your only son, whom it has been convened to celebrate

LICHAS has handed OEDIPUS a piece of paper with some news on it – as he reads it, everyone goes quiet.

JOCASTA   What does it say?

OEDIPUS hands her the paper.

             I have no idea where my glasses are – Corin! – and there is no way I could

OEDIPUS   Early signs, looking good.

JOCASTA   Good.

JOCASTA taps a glass with a spoon –

             Everyone, here we all are. Tonight. An evening off.

OEDIPUS   It sounds like a *lifetime*

JOCASTA   And tonight is really all about one man, one glorious, wonderful man, who I know – is one of the most important men in my life, in all of our lives, and to my mind, one of the most important human beings in the world –

             …OEDIPUS – *is the expectation…*

             This will be Corin's final meal with us

Attention swings round to CORIN – the family laugh, cheer, applaud.

MEROPE   Tonight?

CORIN	I'm afraid so. Putting the old boy out to pasture.
JOCASTA	We begged him not to retire – begged him to stay
MEROPE	After how many years' service?
CORIN	Fifty-five
MEROPE	And where are you from? Originally?
OEDIPUS	Release your birth certificate, Corin, it's the only way –
ETEOCLES	Corin, Nana is interviewing you for your next job
POLYNEICES	as her bitch
OEDIPUS	Thank you, gentlemen
ETEOCLES	That / wasn't me!
CORIN	It's a village, tiny handful of houses, north of the wild forest at the base of the mountain. Haven't lived there for years, but –
MEROPE	That's very near where our home was, our first / cottage –
OEDIPUS	yes
CORIN	I didn't realise that! My parents lived up there –
MEROPE	No longer?
CORIN	No longer living anywhere
MEROPE	I'm sorry.
CORIN	Ah, they were old. I used to go back there whenever there was trouble, pay my respects.

It's a peaceful part of the world. I was sorry to hear about your / husband

MEROPE　　　Yes, he's sorry he's not able to be with us.

Momentary awkwardness, ANTIGONE *rescues it –*

ANTIGONE　　We're going to miss you, Corin

CORIN　　　　I've stayed too long, really, hanging on past the time I should have gone, but your mother said: see out the campaign – and I thought, what's one more year?

MEROPE　　　Do you not have a wife?

CORIN　　　　I don't

ANTIGONE　　(*to* MEROPE) You interested?

OEDIPUS　　　Not appropriate –

But the look on MEROPE's *face is enough to silence* ANTIGONE: MEROPE *is thinking of her husband.* JOCASTA *might secretly find this quite funny.* CORIN *smoothly picks up as if there hasn't been the interruption.*

At some point around here – OEDIPUS *will try and get a cigarette,* JOCASTA *will take it from him and put it in the water pitcher so he can't smoke it.*

CORIN　　　　And I used to say to this one [JOCASTA], when she was a very young woman indeed, before she was married, before she had any of you [children], I said, I would do anything for you.

,

And I hope I have.

JOCASTA　　　You have. You absolutely have.

MEROPE *slightly briskly cuts through this –*

MEROPE	And when do you officially resign?
CORIN	I have already. This is borrowed time.
JOCASTA	A final night, the last full stop on a very full chapter of our lives –
CORIN	You'll do well from tomorrow to find time for a family meal.
OEDIPUS	And doing well is what we do well – and though these two will be off on their voyages of learning, before the year is up, I will have it passed into *law* that they come back home, with boyfriends and girlfriends, and husbands and wives, and then grandchildren after that.
ETEOCLES	Dad, sometimes, I forget that it's possible for you to be silent
OEDIPUS	And how is the girl – name, name, name, I forget / her name
ETEOCLES	(*fast*) She's fine
POLYNEICES	She left him
OEDIPUS MEROPE	(*chorus*) Really? (*chorus*) Why?
ETEOCLES	Fuck off
JOCASTA	language
ETEOCLES	seriously fuck off
JOCASTA	It's not a particularly kind way to behave to your brother
POLYNEICES	He didn't behave a particularly kind way to his girlfriend
ETEOCLES	oh come / on

MEROPE	what?
JOCASTA	(*to* MEROPE) Could / we leave it?
MEROPE	I am a part of the / conversation
POLYNEICES	He cheated on her.

,

JOCASTA	Is that true?
ETEOCLES	It is not anyone at this table's business, is it? what I do in a private relationship, it's – People do things for a REASON.
POLYNEICES	'and I will try my best to think of a reason for what I did'
JOCASTA	Is it true?
OEDIPUS	Now come on –
ANTIGONE	(*to* JOCASTA) Dad's cheated on you.

,

OEDIPUS	What?
ANTIGONE	Most men do. Women put up with it.
OEDIPUS	I'm not most men

This next section fast until OEDIPUS' *explanation* –

JOCASTA	He's your father, not your brother. For God's sake, speak to him with / some respect
OEDIPUS	It's all right –
POLYNEICES	Yeah, it's not like brothers merit respect
CREON	You're not the only person who thinks *that*
OEDIPUS	Respect needs to be earned.

JOCASTA	(*to* ANTIGONE) I don't understand what this latest childhood tantrum is about – I really / don't
ANTIGONE	He's not god though, is he? He isn't actually the perfect / man
MEROPE	I would never have permitted any child of mine to speak to her father in the way you have, young lady.
ANTIGONE	I'm not sure / why that's relevant
OEDIPUS	It's all right. I haven't, actually, Antigone. And – look, it's not that in twenty-three years of marriage, you're not tempted, or there aren't opportunities, it's because your one person is worth so much more than that. We're all part animal, part angel, and the animal is tempted every time, but the pleasure is overcoming it, reaching for something purer and higher – and love is a knowledge / that
ETEOCLES	Dad, if this is heading towards the story of how you two first met and how you were speaking in front of a tiny crowd, you'd tried to cancel the speech and then afterwards / she came up
POLYNEICES	Mum talked to you and from the first / hello, you both just knew
ETEOCLES	you both just knew – immediately the first moment, and Mum / bought you the first expensive champagne you'd ever had and you stayed up talking to each other
ANTIGONE	brought the first proper champagne you'd ever tasted
E/P/A	all night
JOCASTA	Actually, it wasn't all talking –

A microbeat. JOCASTA *and* OEDIPUS *feel the urge to laugh – and push each other on –*

> There was something of a rush to find a hotel room –

ANTIGONE   Nobody wants to hear it

JOCASTA   It's your origin story, darling –

ANTIGONE   My *what*?

OEDIPUS   You wouldn't be here if all we'd done that night is talk –

The kids groan. ETEOCLES *gestures 'We're eating!'*

> Oh come on – it's a natural thing!

MEROPE   What it's not is an appropriate topic of conversation

JOCASTA   Every animal does it.

MEROPE   Animals do plenty of things we'd never allow.

JOCASTA   Such as having sex?

MEROPE   Such as killing each other and eating the corpses –

OEDIPUS   Yes but why are we embarrassed about love? Because someone once decided, and blindly we follow, they decided the things we really want should be the things about which we feel shame. And love is the thing everyone wants – *everyone.*

He looks around the table at each person.

> It's not embarrassing. It's the only thing that matters in the end, how much love? how much were you worth? – how much did you receive, and how much did you give, and how

	much did you risk for it, how bold were you, how brave? And when your person reaches out and takes your hand, the one you feel no shame about being naked with, at home inside their body like it is an extension of your own, when you and they embark on creating life together –
MEROPE	Stop talking, Oedipus
OEDIPUS	Come on, you have felt this too – you and Granddad / – to lift up from yourselves a new person, with arms and toes and lungs, there was *nothing*, and now there's a person
MEROPE	You don't know that
MEROPE	Stop talking, Oedipus, it's not appropriate
OEDIPUS	Love isn't appropriate; it isn't ruled by *manners*, I'm trying to say there is a colossal, chaotic kind of beauty to this one-in-a-million chance / – that these
MEROPE	This is not the time for a speech. Your father's on his deathbed and I'm not in the mood.
	,
	(*to* ETEOCLES) It's a disappointing thing you've done.
ETEOCLES	I know. I didn't bring it up for public trial.
MEROPE	Regardless. It's disappointing.
OEDIPUS	(*to* ETEOCLES) But *why* did you do it?
ETEOCLES	What is this, group / therapy?
MEROPE	As if 'why' makes the slightest bit of difference.
OEDIPUS	No, my young men will understand that they

have *feelings* – I don't want strange, sullen creatures only interested in sports and alcohol and repressing rage. We don't raise men like that in this family.

MEROPE Like your father, you mean?

JOCASTA What is going on with you two tonight?

OEDIPUS Nothing. There's nothing wrong. We're just all at high pressure. Aren't we, Mum?

MEROPE *does not reply, continues eating.*

ANTIGONE How is Granddad?

MEROPE *does not reply.*

OEDIPUS He's the same.

POLYNEICES Corin, do you have to hand in the gun?

CORIN God! Yes, I do, in fact I should have done it this morning but I forgot –

As CORIN *pats his holster, panicky, he realises that* ETEOCLES *has stolen the gun from him –*

ETEOCLES put your HANDS UP

MEROPE (*chorus*) Oh for crying out loud –
JOCASTA (*chorus*) Corin, *please*, I don't like that thing at the table

OEDIPUS It's perfectly / safe –

CORIN Please, everyone, there is no need to worry – it is really perfectly safe, it isn't *loaded* – (*he realises*) oh, God, it *is* loaded – right, fine, I will put it *in / the safe*

JOCASTA the safe and lock the door, *please.*

CORIN *goes off to get rid of the gun.*

MEROPE My *God*

POLYNEICES (*to* MEROPE) It's hilarious: he has to carry it because he's officially Mum's bodyguard but Mum doesn't think she / needs a bodyguard so was happy for it to be Corin

JOCASTA Nobody needs a whole story about it – / can we please put it away

POLYNEICES I think we have forgotten that Eteocles *has cheated on his girlfriend* –

JOCASTA No, we hadn't forgotten, I think we thought it might be kinder not to air the details of Eteocles' private life in public conversation

OEDIPUS And in case you thought I hadn't picked up there was trouble from the way you [ETEOCLES] said no when I asked you if you were bringing anyone to the party tonight – though of course, you [POLYNEICES] also said no, but in a very speedy way indeed, as if there was nobody at all in your life, and you think you slipped that one past me, but nobody slips anything past me, because I know that there is in fact a someone in your life – I don't have a name, granted, but I do know that the someone is another young *man* which disappoints / me –

POLYNEICES why the fuck did you / tell him that?

ANTIGONE I didn't tell him / anything! I didn't

POLYNEICES you're a fucking cunt. *Cunt.*

MEROPE (!) if I had called my sister that word, my mother would have skinned me / alive

POLYNEICES Nobody wants a history / lesson

OEDIPUS *Thank you* – I was going to say, that disappoints me in three ways: one, that any atom in your body was scared I would do anything other than love you and accept you, two that you thought this family might have any other reaction than delight – and three that you didn't bring him here to meet us tonight, while there's still time. And if there is a bit of you that thinks that anyone except you has a right to decide how you love – well [obviously that's not true].

[If] you find your person – whoever, whatever they are, you find them – and our only reply is our joy. Our *only* reply.

Polyneices, we drink to you.

The family drink to **POLYNEICES**.

This is allowed to settle, and then he picks up his glass. Taps a spoon on it.

OEDIPUS Corin, you have been like a father to my radiant wife since she was a radiant girl. We're sorry to lose you, but you'll be back to see us, I'm sure. Enjoy your retirement. Take some time. Our gratitude.

The family drink to **CORIN**.

I want to say something too about my father. He worked with his hands, with the trees and he made beautiful, simple things. It was a simple life – but / it

MEROPE 'was'

OEDIPUS what?

MEROPE 'WAS', as if he's already dead. He is still alive. He is still alive.

OEDIPUS   What is wrong with you?

MEROPE   You know. You know what's wrong.

Microbeat of OEDIPUS' *confusion.*

               It's all over.

OEDIPUS   What?

MEROPE   The first time I've come to see you *on my own.* Your famous emotional intelligence only extends so far – yes, you're about to step into a new life – but, you know what? So am I. So is every other person at this table.

OEDIPUS   I know, Mum

MEROPE   You do not know. You do NOT KNOW, and you have never known. And even if you're ashamed of your parents, they are *nonetheless your parents*. And *you* [JOCASTA] can try and exclude me from a family celebration, keep me on the wrong side of the secret, but you will not exclude me from my son.

MEROPE leaves the table and the room.

JOCASTA   What's going on?

OEDIPUS   I don't know.

JOCASTA   that isn't like her. And you're on edge too.

OEDIPUS doesn't want to talk in front of CREON. The family continue to eat, but then ANTIGONE taps a spoon to her glass.

               Oh God –

ANTIGONE   I want to say something too.

               Whatever anyone else does, tonight is an incredible achievement, Dad. Whatever the

	result, it's been an amazing thing to watch, this campaign, it's the best thing I've ever been near. And when it goes the way we hope it will, I wanted to say, surprise us. Make brave things happen.
JOCASTA	Is this your role to play?
ANTIGONE	What?
JOCASTA	Perhaps you might have thought 'it isn't quite right for me to make a toast to Dad, perhaps that's Mum's place, and that's something / she might have liked'
ANTIGONE	Oh for God's sake, everything has to come back to fucking you

ANTIGONE *gets up and leaves the room.*

JOCASTA	I can't say anything to her at the moment, I don't know where it comes from.

,

CREON	Seeing as we're all getting up

CREON *gets up and makes for the door.*

OEDIPUS	Sit down. Sit *down*.
CREON	Need more time to work out how this is my fault?
OEDIPUS	You're a liar. And you've made your own bed.

CREON *loses his composure.*

CREON	Fuck you, Oedipus – you know what? – Fuck you.
CORIN	(*chorus*) Come on, gentlemen, let's give them some space, / come on
JOCASTA	(*chorus*) What's going on?

CORIN *takes* POLYNEICES *and* ETEOCLES *out.*
It's just JOCASTA, OEDIPUS *and* CREON – *whose conversation has continued unabated* –

OEDIPUS   Your brother set a little trap for me this evening. Brings in some fortune-teller with a handful of predictions – top of the bill, that Creon will win tonight's election. Not difficult to find the underlying story *there* – but he's also been briefed to / deliver

CREON   He won't / listen – none of this actually happened

JOCASTA   Sorry, what did he say? What were the predictions?

OEDIPUS   (*ongoing*) A riddle, something that turns everything round but stands still itself. That I killed your first husband. And that I am destined to murder my father and sleep with my mother.

,

JOCASTA *bursts out laughing.*

JOCASTA   And *why* is that a problem? It's ridiculous – it is a *joke*, is what it is – and why would Creon do that? Creon was worried because you announced the investigation idea –

OEDIPUS   It isn't an idea. It is happening.

CREON   Yes, but when you decided to announce it / without knowing it, you inserted yourself into a complex situation –

JOCASTA   Creon
JOCASTA   *Creon*

CREON   He's already won: the accident, / all of it, is coming to him tomorrow anyway, there's no way he doesn't end up *knowing*

OEDIPUS	No
JOCASTA	But let's not open that up now – *tomorrow*
OEDIPUS	The accident?
CREON	The second he's in post, he has access to every piece of classified / information
JOCASTA	I know that – but it isn't / necessary *tonight*
OEDIPUS	Fuck you.
	,
CREON	What?
OEDIPUS	(*to* CREON) You know about the accident?
CREON	yes
OEDIPUS	You've managed to dig that out. You really have planned your attack on me, haven't you?
	(*to* JOCASTA) You wouldn't have told him. Tell me you didn't –
JOCASTA	What?
CREON	Oedipus, / when you made that announcement
OEDIPUS	I have no idea how something that happened when I was – *eighteen* years old –
JOCASTA	Oedipus, what Creon is saying, or trying to say, is that the reason we're nervous about your investigation into the truth of Laius' death is that we both know the truth of Laius' death.
	We both have, have had for years, the – / clearances, the permissions, thank you, that allow / us
CREON	the permissions

OEDIPUS	It wasn't a heart attack
JOCASTA	No.
OEDIPUS	I should have been told
JOCASTA	We have just told you, boyo
OEDIPUS	*Before*
JOCASTA	We did tell you / before
OEDIPUS	Before I head out there and do a whole fucking thing about digging into what I think must be the groundless speculation about it being a cover-up, and what turns out to be the completely fucking true speculation about a cover-up which / actually took place
JOCASTA	You're not elected yet. And it was thirty years ago.
OEDIPUS	It is going to *seem like I knew.*
	Sorry. This isn't your / fault
JOCASTA	It really isn't my fault. Nor is it his [CREON].

OEDIPUS *looks behind him to check it's safe to speak.*

OEDIPUS	How did they kill him?
JOCASTA	No, they didn't kill him – / he
CREON	It was an *accident on the road*, that's what I was saying.
OEDIPUS	What accident?!

They look at each other. That's a strange coincidence.

JOCASTA	Right. There is the accident Laius died in, and there is the accident that Oedipus had when he was a child. Different things.

CREON	Oedipus, when was that?
OEDIPUS	I was a child – eighteen?
CREON	You never mentioned this.
OEDIPUS	Not to you.
JOCASTA	Let's not / get into that now
OEDIPUS	Listen, I was in an accident on the roads when I was a child, and yes, I am lucky to be alive, and no, nobody was killed. And it says something about you that you think / it's something that needs –
JOCASTA	Creon, could this be a problem?
CREON	I don't know what 'this' is. When did Laius die?
JOCASTA	thirty… four (?) years ago?
OEDIPUS	When I was eighteen. , Are you suggesting that the two accidents –
CREON	Tell me what happened.
OEDIPUS	Why?
JOCASTA	(*to* OEDIPUS) Stop being a child. Just tell him. You were out on the road, going too fast – ,
OEDIPUS	I used to enjoy – when I was young – I loved driving at speed. I saw them, a speck ahead of me in the distance and I wanted to overtake – and so I clamped my foot down, and I soared after them, only, suddenly the other car was

coming *towards* me. I don't know how it had happened, I was going the wrong way, had been going the wrong way for miles

CREON And then?

OEDIPUS It was head-on – and then nothing and I remember going under – thinking, this is dying.

Did they investigate Laius' death? At the time –

CREON Please – go on – you went under, and –

OEDIPUS And then I wake up and I see this man is dragging me out of the car, I thought a doctor or something – and then he pulls me up so I'm looking into his face – and he says, get out of here. Forget you were ever here. Turn around and run and don't look back. Sun low in the sky behind him, he's a silhouette, [bald head], I can't see his face, and I see the man lying on my windscreen, thrown clean through the glass, up out of the passenger seat. I thought he was dead.

We'll deal with him, we'll tend to him, run away, the first man says again. And I did.

CREON And were you hurt?

OEDIPUS Bruised, that's all. None of the blood on me was mine –

CREON And you didn't think to say anything about this during the campaign?

Did you tell anyone?

OEDIPUS I got home, I told my parents everything. We called hospitals, police, anywhere we could think of, and asked – any fatal accidents.

	Any accidents. *Anything*. Nothing. No deaths announced.
CREON	And why do you think that is? But you haven't spoken to anyone since? Did your parents tell / anyone?
OEDIPUS	Why would they do that?
CREON	So you didn't try and cover it up?
OEDIPUS	There was nothing to cover up – it was an *accident*
CREON	Where did your accident happen?
OEDIPUS	Where the road out of the city splits, it's a three-way – there are three roads that come together –
JOCASTA	But that's not how Laius died.
OEDIPUS	It's not?
JOCASTA	That's not how Laius died. He sat in the back of the car, not the front. Think about it. Just like you, he had his driver. And there were three people in the other car.
	,
CREON	Okay. Thank fuck for that. Are you sure?
JOCASTA	He was my husband.
OEDIPUS	But how do you know there were three men?
JOCASTA	Laius' driver witnessed it. He was sworn to secrecy, but –
OEDIPUS	Tell me the three men in the other car are still alive –
	,

JOCASTA	I don't know –

JOCASTA *looks at* CREON. *He doesn't know either.*

OEDIPUS	If the man in the car I hit was Laius –
JOCASTA	It wasn't
OEDIPUS	If the man in the car I hit was Laius –
CREON	Should I get the team back here? There might be something here we have to / handle
OEDIPUS	No, let them be. Just the three of us. For now. If we need them later, then fine. But if [it was Laius] –
CREON	I'll find him. Laius' driver. I don't think the two accidents *can* be the same
JOCASTA	There were three people in the car that killed Laius!
CREON	– but we should make sure. For your peace of mind, if nothing else.
OEDIPUS	Yes. Thank you. And / not a word
CREON	Don't worry. I'll go now.

Exit CREON.

JOCASTA	My word not good enough?
OEDIPUS	This is my whole life. If it turns out the two things are the same
JOCASTA	That's absurd, Oedipus
OEDIPUS	That man said I killed Laius.
JOCASTA	which is impossible.
OEDIPUS	We don't know that.

JOCASTA	Laius was in the back seat. Your man was in the front. There were three people in the car that hit Laius. You're impressive, yes, but you're not three people.
OEDIPUS	The coincidence doesn't worry you at all? Two accidents, similar accidents, the same *time*, and a prediction that I killed Laius.
JOCASTA	There's only one thing I worry about
OEDIPUS	What?
JOCASTA	After you've sorted this out, how will we stop you doing the deed with my beloved mother-in-law?
OEDIPUS	This isn't funny
JOCASTA	It is quite funny
OEDIPUS	This is my *whole fucking life*
JOCASTA	No, this is your anxiety expressing itself on the night you become the most powerful man in the country, expressing itself in things which are frankly absurd, and being / so
OEDIPUS	If that was true, I'd lose – everything
JOCASTA	Including your sense of humour, apparently. Everyone's *tense* tonight. Except me.
	Look, every man has the fucking his mother dream at some point. It is par for the course.
OEDIPUS	It wasn't a [dream] – I really don't understand why this amuses you so much.

He is amused, though, almost infectiously now –

JOCASTA	Oh you have to laugh – don't you? – you have to laugh you have to laugh you have to laugh

Enter LICHAS.

LICHAS — I wanted to check if you needed anything?

JOCASTA — Oh so many things

OEDIPUS — Ignore her. It's the champagne.

JOCASTA — It depends what you're offering

OEDIPUS — We're fine. Thank you. Any news?

LICHAS — Crowds are there already. Despite the weather.

OEDIPUS — Is it raining?

LICHAS — Not yet. Any minute.

OEDIPUS — Thanks.

Exit LICHAS.

Embarrassment. You are an embarrassment.

JOCASTA — Well. You have to release the pressure somehow. Big night.

They look at each other, challenging. She unbuttons his shirt, or slips a hand onto his groin – and eventually, they kiss, and then kiss hungrily.

And let's not pretend you haven't thought about her [LICHAS]. Tight little bud like that, young and nubile and available to bloom at a moment's notice –

OEDIPUS — I only have eyes for you – and let's not pretend you don't know it

He runs at her, maybe there's a bit of a play-fight, he lifts her up – puts her down onto a sofa – kneels down in front of her, starts to unbutton or unzip what she's wearing – she doesn't resist –

JOCASTA — Wait –

She produces a book of matches –

OEDIPUS   Are they?

JOCASTA   The ones from the first hotel, yes they are. I'm going to light a candle. It's a moment to mark.

OEDIPUS   I thought it was just for moments for 'us'?

JOCASTA   If this isn't a moment for us, I don't know what is –

OEDIPUS   You don't want to wait until I've formally accepted?

JOCASTA   No, I don't want to wait.

OEDIPUS   I don't want to jinx it.

JOCASTA *lights a candle – a moment while they look at it.*

How many are left?

JOCASTA   Enough. Well, how many do we need, now? No more children to come. A thirtieth wedding anniversary. A fortieth. And one for you to light beside my dead body –

OEDIPUS   *Don't* – I really really don't want you to die – you can't die

JOCASTA   Then you should never have married somebody so many thousands of years older than you

OEDIPUS   Don't –

JOCASTA   Seriously you should have thought about that

OEDIPUS   Don't – don't – don't –

He holds her, kisses her –

	I love you.
	It's all to impress you, you know. All of it.
JOCASTA	Well, supreme leader, so long as you remember that, when in [TIME] or whatever, when you have an international portfolio of interests, that you have very specific responsibilities in negotiating my particular area of – shall we call it domestic policy? –
OEDIPUS	Oh this particular area will remain at the top of the list – there is no one before you –
JOCASTA	And if the demands of sexy young attendants beating at the doors and and your sexy old mother in the very next room, and the sexy prophecies that let you have your wicked way without / taking any responsibility – that's it, actually, the lack of responsibility

They start to have oral sex, him on her.

OEDIPUS	You're not going to put me off – there's / no stopping me now
JOCASTA	When was there ever any use trying to stop *you*, I wouldn't waste my time trying to stop [you] –

But at that moment words fail her –

ohhh baby

They continue. It should feel loving, not embarrassing.

And then the door opens – OEDIPUS *gets up very fast – half caught –*

ANTIGONE	(*chorus*) Dada?
OEDIPUS	(*chorus*) hello, baby

It's ANTIGONE, *unaware.* JOCASTA *remains slightly hidden, setting herself right.*

ANTIGONE   They want to come in and take the furniture out. Can they?

OEDIPUS   Yeah, yes – in a minute –

ANTIGONE   (*off*) in a minute

(*to* OEDIPUS) I remember Creon when we first came in here, all that time, where to put the walls up and choosing furniture and who sits where. Everything we put in, carried out wrapped in plastic.

OEDIPUS   Yes. But a whole new beginning beyond this place.

ANTIGONE   What he said to you, before, the predictions –

OEDIPUS   Don't worry about it, sweetie.

ANTIGONE   I thought you didn't want to involve those people; I thought you didn't believe in any of that.

OEDIPUS   I don't –

ANTIGONE   So why was he here?

OEDIPUS   Because your uncle trusts people too much – but, look, clearly, he's not well –

ANTIGONE   It made me feel sick. You sent him out and he cried – Dad, he / cried

OEDIPUS   He's a joke.

ANTIGONE   Dad, what if he's right?

JOCASTA *appears, re-dressed.*

JOCASTA   Why are we so obsessed with staring backwards into the abyss?

ANTIGONE *ignores* JOCASTA, *speaks to* OEDIPUS.

OEDIPUS 63

ANTIGONE   They looked him up. He's called Teiresias. He's been right before.

OEDIPUS   And he's been wrong. Like all of us.

ANTIGONE   But Dad –

JOCASTA   Oh stop it. You're not a child any more.

ANTIGONE   I hate the way you say that.

JOCASTA   Hate it as much as you like, you're not [a child].

ANTIGONE   You mean, you're not a mother any more. Or you don't want to be. That's actually what you mean.

JOCASTA   when you're old enough to vote, my work is *done.*

Enter LICHAS.

LICHAS   I'm sorry to interrupt but your mother was asking / whether it might be possible

Enter MEROPE, *shortly behind.*

MEROPE   Your mother was asking when you were planning on delivering on your promise of some actual time / with you

OEDIPUS   Later. Not right now. Not right now – I'm sorry, I'm just busy with something.

JOCASTA   We'll need to go. Won't we?

OEDIPUS *works out what this code means.*

OEDIPUS   Yes. We're actually late for head, head of state, an important call of – conference call, through there, could get a little heated – ten minutes

JOCASTA   twenty / minutes

OEDIPUS   twenty minutes

He takes JOCASTA*'s hand.*

          but when we're back, my time is yours –

They leave. When out of the line of fire, perhaps we see them laughing. They're really great together.

MEROPE   Children find themselves so mysterious. But a mother knows.

ANTIGONE   He seems on edge.

MEROPE   It's the waiting. He's neither one thing nor the other now, until the country gives its verdict, and no matter how hard he pushes, it will come at its own pace.

ANTIGONE   Yeah.

          I keep thinking, when he steps into that new position, I keep thinking about what all of *us* become. From tomorrow morning, that's the headline on my obituary: 'Daughter of Oedipus'. I mean, when he chose to run, he chose that for all of us.

MEROPE   He breathes a lot of oxygen. Always has. But you have his determination. You haven't touched your book all night.

ANTIGONE   It's been pretty busy –

MEROPE   The reason you brought it isn't to read it. It's to remind him that there's things he doesn't know. Which tells me, you'll be fine.

ANTIGONE   It's nice that you're here. I feel... nervous. I think. You should come more often. He really isn't ashamed of you, you / know

MEROPE	I know he isn't.

,

ANTIGONE	How's Granddad?
MEROPE	When we were eating, they were trying to call but there's not an answer now.
ANTIGONE	I'm sure it's nothing –
MEROPE	Only one thing it can be, in the end.

,

ANTIGONE	Are you afraid?
MEROPE	He's stubborn. If there's a way, provided he wants to, that man will survive anything.
ANTIGONE	His father's son. No, his… son's father. I don't know.

,

MEROPE	The wind's up.
	I'm sorry if I snapped at you at the table. What you said about your parents' marriage.
ANTIGONE	It's all right (?)
MEROPE	Your grandfather had a woman.

This is unexpected.

ANTIGONE	Before you?
MEROPE	At the same time.
	I know. Why didn't I leave? But what you don't understand yet is what love can do to you. How deep its roots go down. How completely it smashes the walls.

ANTIGONE   But didn't it make you sad?

MEROPE   It made me – disillusioned. Two people can live inside an illusion. Add a third – and the curtain comes down. And the idea of starting again, what could be worse? Painting over your memories with new ones.

And I still loved him.

You'll find out.

CORIN comes in with a team, they take some of the furniture.

ANTIGONE   I don't know. I can't imagine what comes next.

MEROPE   None of us ever know. It only ever catches up with you afterwards. By my age, from the other side, you know a little more – who you are, what it was for, where you went wrong – and your very best people step out of the picture, never to come back. I think, once you know, that means it's ending. Knowledge in advance is the gift of the gods.

ANTIGONE   I don't believe in gods, I don't think

MEROPE   Makes no difference whether you believe in them or not. Just because you don't see it, doesn't mean it isn't happening. Your generation think the world began when you did.

ANTIGONE   Yours think it should end when you do.

MEROPE smiles at her granddaughter. CREON comes in, flustered.

CREON   Sorry – is Oedipus in here?

MEROPE   Are you worried he might be invisible?

CREON	There's someone here to see him.
MEROPE	Join the queue.
CREON	It's important.
MEROPE	He isn't here. (!)
CREON	I need him – actually both of them – Corin, where are they?
MEROPE	I should call again [about my husband].
CORIN	I don't know – I don't know where they are
CREON	Can you *find* them?
CORIN	I can try my best.

Exit CORIN. CREON *sits down.*

MEROPE	He's in love with your mother, that man.
ANTIGONE	Corin? Do you think?
MEROPE	You look, you see. It's in his eyes.

Exit MEROPE. *It's now just* CREON *and* ANTIGONE. ANTIGONE *picks up her book from where it was left earlier.*

ANTIGONE	Bad night?
CREON	Not great, to be honest.
	I mean, the result is great, obviously

She smiles.

                  You know how it is.

ANTIGONE	Yup.
	Do you think things really are going to change?

CREON   Big question. Do you?

ANTIGONE   I'd love to hope that they will. I think if I look at it all, and knowing what Dad's like with everything, then yes. But I don't *feel* it.

I don't know. Maybe you don't [feel it].

What I do know is that I don't feel like doing *this*.

She puts the book down.

I sometimes think, the thing that stops you setting out on a particular road is that you might get nearly to the end and then find some tiny, seemingly irrelevant thing that in reality punctures everything you've done and empties it of all its meaning. Like if I knew why I was doing this, if I knew where this would lead me, I might never start doing it.

CREON *picks the book up.*

CREON   'What has four legs in the morning, two in the afternoon and three by nightfall?'

It's us, isn't it – crawling, walking, walking stick?

ANTIGONE   But what does it mean? 'A single day's events can make you old'? Or – 'people change'? Or 'you don't learn to walk, you only hold the skill for a brief time and then it slips away'? Or 'humans are animals'? And surely some old people end up on their hands and knees again –

It's pretending to be this tidy, neat example and actually it's just a window onto how everything is open chaos. Uncontainable. It's like opening the door on a room you're supposed to tidy and finding that the walls are on fire.

CREON   I'd say it's 'everyone bows to the laws in the end'.

ANTIGONE   But that's what you believe anyway, isn't it? You've just seen yourself in it.

CREON   Maybe. But maybe there's a certain way things should be. Have to be.

ANTIGONE   In which case, do whatever you like. Have a *party*. Take your clothes off. You can't avoid where it's going, it was always going there, everyone ends up dead, so may as well have the wildest available journey.

CREON   Maybe that's the solution the riddle yields to. Everyone ends up dead.

ANTIGONE   Maybe it doesn't ever yield to a single solution.

She shuts the book.

               Why choose one?

CREON   Nature of life, I guess. And elections. Keeps things simple.

               I like what you're wearing.

The tension between CREON *and* ANTIGONE *is charged. Perhaps something is about to happen… interrupted by applause from the back room – and cheers.* OEDIPUS *and* JOCASTA *have come in and there's a broadcast on the screen. People are hugging.*

OEDIPUS *and* JOCASTA *come through –*

ANTIGONE   What is it?

CREON   Exit polls.

ANTIGONE   And?

JOCASTA   Landslide.

ANTIGONE looks at CREON.

CREON   (*to* OEDIPUS) Where did you go?

JOCASTA   He wasn't feeling well. He's feeling better.

CREON   I found our man. I'll bring him through.

CREON gets the DRIVER. As he comes in, he's really astonished to be in a room with OEDIPUS and JOCASTA.

JOCASTA   Antigone, can we have the room, please?

Exit ANTIGONE. OEDIPUS focuses his attention.

CREON   (*to the* DRIVER) Sit there.

                 We need to ask you some questions, in confidence. I'm afraid we can't tell you why, we're not going to tell you why, but we need you to be absolutely honest. Everything you remember.

JOCASTA   The night my first husband died, you were driving the car. Yes?

DRIVER   Yes. Please, I / don't want to

JOCASTA   It's all right. I know what you swore, you're safe. *I'm* asking you. We need you to tell us what happened, what *really* happened, not the story we put out, who sat where, whatever you can remember –

DRIVER   It was an off-the-record trip. It was summer, early evening. We were going to a hotel, big place out beyond the limits of the city, he was late and he was beside me, kept rapping his hand on the dashboard, impatient.

JOCASTA   beside you?

DRIVER   Your husband was in the front seat next to me.

                  ,

CREON   Why would he be in the front seat?

DRIVER   He wanted to smoke and the windows don't
                  come down in the back – same as now, they're
                  bulletproof, fixed solid. For safety, in case
                  someone were to / try

JOCASTA   Yes

DRIVER   I told him it was against the protocol for
                  him to sit in the front with me. But he was
                  angry I'd even said anything, climbing into
                  the front seat, turning the music off. Sitting
                  there, right next to me, no seatbelt, smoking
                  cigarette after cigarette, swearing, spitting
                  bits of tobacco out of the window, it was late
                  summer, he was in a tremendous hurry – and
                  we were coming along the outskirts of the city,
                  where the three roads meet –

OEDIPUS   It's the same thing

JOCASTA   Go on. *Go on.*

DRIVER   The other car came out of nowhere, just
                  where the three roads meet, flashed at us fast,
                  horn screaming and I stamped on the brake,
                  but too late – they were going like lightning,
                  hit us so hard the back wheels came up off the
                  ground.

                  They're such quiet roads, normally, I wasn't
                  watching, I didn't / see

OEDIPUS   *It's the same thing.*

JOCASTA   (*to* OEDIPUS) Three people. Three people.

CREON   Would you recognise any of the people in the other car?

DRIVER   What?

CREON   The car that crashed into yours. There were three people / in it

DRIVER   No

,

He senses this atmosphere, unsure why it's been created.

Just one. The crash hurled Laius through the windscreen, head-first at the other car. He's half-slumped on the bonnet, broken neck, dead on impact. Kid saw that, was in shock, he just – he wasn't hurt, he ran for it. And the rest you know.

CREON   You're sure there weren't three / people

DRIVER   There were three of us *at the scene*. Well. Two of us, and – [a body]. Well, it was just me, really, the kid fled

OEDIPUS   So didn't you arrest him? Were there no doctors?

DRIVER   The protocol was not to call the police. Laius' trip was – unofficial: it was off-schedule, you know –

JOCASTA   Yes. Thank you, but what did you do?

DRIVER   I made an evaluation myself that Laius was already dead. I made a phone call and I was told not to do anything, to wait.

It's not my place to reveal secrets.

OEDIPUS	Clearly.
DRIVER	I'm paid to drive the car. I trusted they had good reasons for what they said. It's not my place.
OEDIPUS	It is all of our place to seek the truth in the face of lies
DRIVER	In this instance, sir, it wasn't my confidence to break. Any more than if you gave me instructions now. We all serve one agenda. Then, that belonged to Laius. Now it belongs to you.
OEDIPUS	Well we'll see, won't we.
	How long do I have?
CREON	[TIME]
OEDIPUS	I think you can go now
DRIVER	Have I done something wrong?
JOCASTA	Have you told anyone this story?
DRIVER	No
JOCASTA	Your wife?
DRIVER	I'm not married
CREON	Would you recognise him? The driver of the other car?
	,
DRIVER	He was a boy. It was nearly thirty-five years ago. He'd be a grown man now.
JOCASTA	Thank you for your time. You've been helpful. Don't worry about this, all right?

CREON	I'll show you out
OEDIPUS	No, let her [LICHAS] do it –
	Thank you.

The DRIVER *leaves, shown out by* LICHAS.

	,
	I need a cigarette
JOCASTA	Not in / here
OEDIPUS	Get that man back here. Teiresias. He was right. It's the same – I need to –
JOCASTA	[you need to] *what?*
OEDIPUS	*I don't know.* Find him. Get him back. I mean it, we need to get to the bottom of what is happening here.
JOCASTA	Well, we know where your mother is if you want to get on with step two.
OEDIPUS	Don't. Don't.
JOCASTA	And I don't know about killing your dad, but that's at least six hours' drive from here, and you don't have that sort of time.
OEDIPUS	I killed Laius. That prophecy was *true*.
JOCASTA	In an *accident*.
CREON	*Thirty-five years* ago.
OEDIPUS	I killed your husband. The coincidence doesn't / unsettle you?
JOCASTA	No. No. And no.
	You cannot seriously expect me to believe – *you* cannot seriously believe, someone as intelligent

	and capable and informed as you, that these prophecies have somehow got this right
CREON	Three years of work, a hell of a campaign, we're finally getting somewhere where something can be *done*, and your honesty fetish is going to pull everything apart because some crazed [man] – you cannot be so fucking *naive* –
OEDIPUS	I asked you to go and get Teiresias. Can you please go and get Teiresias?

CREON *exits.*

JOCASTA	What's wrong with you?
OEDIPUS	I destroyed a human life. I took a human life. That's not a small [thing], I took a human life, I killed Laius.
JOCASTA	Again, that was an / *accident* and not a murder
OEDIPUS	YOU HEARD THE STORY. I WAS DRIVING THE WRONG WAY.
JOCASTA	And it is thirty years *gone*. There really is no need to raise your voice
OEDIPUS	So if it isn't prophetic – then HOW DID TEIRESIAS KNOW? – that is what is worrying me / if you need to –
JOCASTA	I'm saying: he must have known that anyway. It's not impossible, is it? There was a cover-up about Laius, yes? that means *people*, *paperwork*, your *name* is somewhere, somewhere *confidential*, tomorrow morning you'll have clearance to see all the information – we'll follow the trail / Teiresias took
OEDIPUS	I'll have to admit it. The cover-up, Laius' death –

JOCASTA   Why?

OEDIPUS   What do you mean *why* – because *that is what happened.*

JOCASTA   So what?

OEDIPUS   So I *took* a *life*. People have a right to know the truth

JOCASTA   No. Wrong. That is not a truth that anyone needs to know. Laius is gone. *You* are what we need: you are on the cusp of changing the whole story. Tonight is the beginning of the million glorious things that *you* are *going to do* – and however you choose to deal with the past, you don't need to do it *tonight* –

OEDIPUS   Lies have consequences.

JOCASTA   This isn't a campaign stop, boyo, and you know as well as I do that we *live* under blankets feathered with lies, the lot of us, everyone, everyone, ev-ery-one *lies*: *politics, government, schools, the facts of the world we live in.* Banknotes and bank loans and half the country's wedding vows – it all turns on lies.

,

OEDIPUS   I killed a human being.

JOCASTA   But nobody knows except us.

OEDIPUS   And then there's *that*: why would they cover it up?

JOCASTA   It was thirty-four years ago. An old man died, / leave it alone

OEDIPUS   But why did they cover it up?

JOCASTA   He was old. He was seventy. And old men die.

OEDIPUS   But *why would they cover it up?* Why not just say there'd been an / accident?

JOCASTA   Is it *important?*

OEDIPUS   Yes – I – I don't understand what difference it would make?

JOCASTA   With a heart attack there was no possibility of blame. No next development. Heart attack? Act of God. The desire was, from everyone, myself included, to seal it tight and drop it to the bottom of the ocean.

Now can we please – *please* – / move on?

OEDIPUS   What do you mean 'it'?

JOCASTA   He wasn't a good man.

OEDIPUS   I know.

JOCASTA   You don't. You *don't.*

But let's leave this.

It has started to rain.

OEDIPUS   You can't say that, and then expect –

,

It isn't easy, you do know it isn't [easy]

JOCASTA   My first marriage is not your problem

OEDIPUS *adopts a newscaster voice:*

OEDIPUS   'It is a remarkable situation, after years of coalition and compromise, that the likely victor of tonight's election is married to the wife of the previous holder of the office: one wonders about political continuity, but that really is a step beyond.'

JOCASTA   I will tell you, Oedipus, but please, not tonight.

OEDIPUS   Jocasta – even if you say it quickly, so I can understand, / that's

JOCASTA   The baby we had. Laius and me, I mean.

OEDIPUS   The one that died.

JOCASTA   Yes.

                Oedipus, I don't want to talk about this now –

                I don't want to *talk about it*.

OEDIPUS   So why not tell the *truth* and there'd be nothing to talk about?

JOCASTA   Oedipus, not telling you isn't lying –

OEDIPUS   I didn't want to have to deal with all of this either.

JOCASTA suddenly throws some of the plates off the table –

and they smash. Or something. But whatever happens here, it's a huge reaction and OEDIPUS *realises as we do that this is more serious for her than it's seemed so far. They're both shocked by it.*

,

JOCASTA   I'm not a liar.

                I don't lie.

                I'm not trying to cover [anything up], but it isn't something I ever wanted to, I mean, I knew one day I would talk to you, but then, why –

She screams or something. Gets herself together.

This way you have of getting things out of me.

All right.

I'm not sure this will ever have occurred to you, but for me to – for me to have gotten pregnant by him, given –

Something in her is resisting this. OEDIPUS *has already moved to comfort her.*

You know what the marriage was like at the end, separate beds, and so on, and you know he was seventy years old when he – when you – when that accident happened. I don't know what's wrong with me, I can hardly speak.

That baby was born – what? – twenty years before his death, which means, when that baby was conceived, he was in his fifties, and I was

OEDIPUS   Fourteen

He's solved it automatically, but it's only as JOCASTA *speaks that he realises:*

JOCASTA   – thirteen

,

And if you think medical science hasn't come a distance, try giving birth twice on either side of twenty-nine years.

OEDIPUS   thirteen

JOCASTA   Unlucky for some

OEDIPUS   But you didn't marry him until –

JOCASTA   The marriage was later.

OEDIPUS	The baby came *after* the marriage –
JOCASTA	I never said that.
OEDIPUS	Thirteen. And no one knew?
JOCASTA	People are good at not knowing. The instinct to look any other direction than the dark. Then, because of him, there were reasons not to know.
OEDIPUS	Thirteen
JOCASTA	And why would a thirteen-year-old girl have sex with an old man? Father issues. But actually? it's not knowing that there's such a thing as *another choice*, the feeling that you have only one possible track –
OEDIPUS	Was it born dead?
JOCASTA	No.
	That would have been a kind of mercy.
	I didn't want to sleep with him. I didn't choose [to] – I don't know if I was the only young girl to receive that – treatment at his hands, but I think now it's highly unlikely. I was too young to know what was being said, and too young to know how to say no, and – well, even when we were married, we slept in separate beds as soon as I was – no longer a child. His face during [sex], furious, mouth-open, smiling –
OEDIPUS	Wait. Laius – Laius
JOCASTA	Laius liked them young. I can't have been the only one, I mean, I *wasn't*, the only one –
	Of course once I'd realised I was expecting (I had no idea what was happening to my body), he said he was in love with me and,

who knows, perhaps he thought he was – and
the marriage, later, of course, once I was old
enough to be married, but now I wonder
whether my father – who was high-up enough
to cause problems for them, too high-up to
simply disappear – whether he didn't have
something to do with Laius' sudden desire to
get married – but my father wasn't exactly
a drink of water either, you never met him,
but take my word for it, my life seems to be
populated by men implosively determined to
get their own way.

OEDIPUS So your father had blackmailed him?

JOCASTA He said he loved me. I don't know. Laius was
terrified of being exposed. But, it doesn't
matter now. It really doesn't matter.

I was three things: a child myself, the mother
of a child, and the lover of a powerful man.
I thought I loved him.

I remember I felt like my body had betrayed
me. Swelling up. Skin going translucent, sort of
purple. Stay the same, I thought. But three months,
six months – (*She gestures 'bigger and bigger'.*)

So. The night they told me Laius was dead
and they suggest we say a heart attack [being
the cause], I didn't ask the questions about
the, *scale* of what they were trying to hide,
about the journey he was taking when he
died, because I didn't want to know the
answer. An off-the-schedule trip to a hotel:
I didn't want to know who else was going
through what I went through. How many of
me there was. What other children were –
I didn't want to wade back through it, the
misery and the secrecy, which makes me a
coward, but sometimes cowardice is exactly
the price of survival –

OEDIPUS	I love you
JOCASTA	I know that.

        His heart. His *heart.* It's quite the irony that *that* was the story.

        So. The rest of it.

        The baby was born. But when the thirteen-year-old who would eventually become his wife became pregnant, way underage, our great leader was very – determined that nobody was going to find out, so I was not allowed to set foot in a hospital, my parents weren't allowed to – there weren't the resources then anyway, and with half a team and meagre equipment and this atmosphere where you could taste the secrecy and shame like bleach in the air – it was an ugly, brutal birth, fluorescent light and forceps and – my body was thin and hard from the anxiety, it was – they damaged my baby, his legs, as they got him out, but it didn't matter because they already knew – they already knew it was going to be – taken away –

        My baby was the evidence of who Laius really was.

        For Laius to do that, to protect his own [reputation] – them prising my hands off this tiny person, vulnerable and bleeding and screaming, they lifted him up and his little toes trailing mucus, all bloodshot, and *they took him away* – to do that to a mother is a *crime*. Yes, he was an unhappy man, people do things for a reason, unconsciously, trying to try and justify the things he did but – but – but that rancid man was a dirty animal and a criminal and when he became a dark-blue plastic bag heavy with fat and old meat, I did not cry a single tear for him.

                    Not like I cried for that boy. I looked at that
                    screaming face in those tiny few minutes
                    I knew him, and he was already so much
                    more to me than my husband, my husband
                    who took me to a dark bed when I was young
                    enough to be his child myself.

OEDIPUS   How could you not have told me this?

This comes from deep inside JOCASTA:

JOCASTA   Oh but WHY? what is the utility of living
                    in the past? Why turn the thing on purpose
                    to look back – at days stretched so full with
                    fear and misery that even the memory is
                    overwhelming? That was a thousand years
                    ago: *this* is my life. I got to here, I made it
                    here. I have a husband, a kind husband, who
                    loves me and whom I love, I have three happy,
                    healthy, well-adjusted children, I have written
                    books and done some good – and now there
                    is the possibility that I can help to change
                    the world, in however small a – I'm saying,
                    I got here in the end, so why focus on the
                    beginning? Who does that help? I don't want
                    to turn it over and over, I don't want to die
                    before it does.

OEDIPUS   And you didn't ask what happened to the
                    child – you / didn't want to know?

JOCASTA   I didn't want to know. Because sometimes we
                    don't, Oedipus, sometimes we don't want to
                    know – we don't ask how sick we are because
                    we know that the answer is *bad*, in exactly the
                    same way you don't ask when the point's going
                    to come that we'll have to flick the switch
                    on your father's machine because, you know
                    what, there is no other possible outcome.

                    It was horrible. However that child died, it
                    was a lonely death.

CREON *enters.*

CREON It's Teiresias –

OEDIPUS I'll be one minute

CREON He isn't here: won't come back.

OEDIPUS He won't / come back?

CREON The message said – 'no return visits'.

,

LICHAS *enters.*

LICHAS Polyneices is outside.

OEDIPUS Give us a moment.

CREON *and* LICHAS *exit.*

OEDIPUS Didn't you talk to a doctor – to / anyone?

JOCASTA I never understood how talking about something makes it hurt any less.

OEDIPUS You could have said something to me.

JOCASTA I think I thought, if I opened my mouth, that my whole life would fall out of it and never go back in again. And those things do not get to be in my life now. I'm fine, on the whole. That man's shadow is no longer pressed against the doorframe when I sleep.

,

So yes, you killed Laius, if that's how you want to put it. That's one side. Turn it over, and you did the world a favour. Mark it up as your greatest achievement. So far.

OEDIPUS   I didn't know

JOCASTA   And still, you did it.

   CORIN *re-enters.*

CORIN   Sorry – can we take some things?

OEDIPUS   One minute –

JOCASTA   No, come in. Come on in. I'm going to have a minute. Take a walk.

She leaves.

More furniture is taken away. POLYNEICES *comes in.*

It's raining.

POLYNEICES   It's nothing major. Wanted to say thanks.

OEDIPUS   For what?

POLYNEICES   Before. What you said – at dinner. About me.

   OEDIPUS *looks up at him.*

OEDIPUS   Nothing to thank me for there.

   OEDIPUS' *thoughts are elsewhere, but he kisses his son on the head.*

POLYNEICES   How are you feeling?

OEDIPUS   Ah, you know. Fine.

POLYNEICES   Strange, waiting for the verdict. The result, I mean.

OEDIPUS   It is.

,

POLYNEICES   Is Mum – ?

OEDIPUS' *thoughts are elsewhere.*

,

OEDIPUS Sorry. Is Mum – ?

POLYNEICES Do you think Mum feels the same as you about – me having a boyfriend?

OEDIPUS I'm sure she does. Ask her –

POLYNEICES No, I – I don't know. It felt like perhaps she didn't approve. She was surprised, I think

OEDIPUS I think she might have known for longer than you have. Did you know at school?

POLYNEICES I don't think I dared know. Children are cruel.

OEDIPUS Everyone's cruel. Children are the only ones who are honest about it. But the world will be different now, the culture will change.

Mothers are complicated. Mine's in a strange old mood tonight as well.

POLYNEICES Because of Granddad? Do you think – do you think she's ready for him to – for it to end?

OEDIPUS People don't have endings. Stories end. People scream 'but I wasn't ready, it wasn't finished, I can do better' –

He snaps his fingers (or something) – as if the voice is abruptly silenced. As if it's the end. As if the lights snap out.

POLYNEICES Yeah.

OEDIPUS You start in the dark. You breathe your way out. You're cut loose from your mother's body and then you wait – until your own body lets you go. And buried at your centre, like the stone in a cherry, a clock winding onward to the end, back to the dark of the very beginning

	And what do we do in between?
POLYNEICES	I – I don't know.

,

OEDIPUS	We try to make things better.

,

	What you've told us tonight – does he make you happy?
POLYNEICES	Yes
OEDIPUS	And have you told the truth about yourself?
POLYNEICES	Yes.
OEDIPUS	That's all you can ever do. You tell the truth.

POLYNEICES *doesn't know it, but* OEDIPUS *has made a decision – or rather, reminded himself of a decision he made for himself a long time ago.*

POLYNEICES	Do you want a drink or something? I might go out and grab a drink.
OEDIPUS	I'm all right. You go.
POLYNEICES	The waiting is… making me nervous, I think.
OEDIPUS	Yes.

Yes it does.

POLYNEICES	You're nervous, aren't you? It's not like you.

You can't lose, you know.

POLYNEICES *goes out.* CREON *comes in.*

CREON	What do you want to do about the Laius situation?

OEDIPUS	Well, my investigation took less time than I thought.
CREON	Yes.
OEDIPUS	And now that I understand the reasons for the cover-up –
CREON	Yes.
OEDIPUS	We'll tell the truth. About who he was. And about what I did.
	I don't know how or when, but we will.
CREON	We can talk about this tomorrow. Take some advice, talk to Jocasta and / work out –
OEDIPUS	I'm going to tell the truth

JOCASTA *comes back in, no knocking.*

JOCASTA	This place is full of people. I only went round in a circle because I managed to forget *this*, and it's a sea of rain out there now –

She's left her bag but, as she gets it, she's left the door open and MEROPE *enters the room.* OEDIPUS *clocks her, misreads her expression as anger.*

OEDIPUS	Mother, I am sorry / I know, I said ten minutes, I said twenty / minutes but there are three million things I'm trying to resolve before / I –
MEROPE	Oedipus
	Oedipus
	Oedipus, he's dead. Your dad.
OEDIPUS	What?
	,
	When?

MEROPE   Just now. Just a few minutes ago.

OEDIPUS   Was it because of me? I mean, he didn't – it wasn't the shock of / the

MEROPE   No, sweetheart, just the cancer. Just the horrid cancer. And he was an old man – and it's one small tip of the scales at his age, and

,

OEDIPUS   I –

                I'm so sorry, Mum

OEDIPUS *embraces* MEROPE.

MEROPE   I'm all right.

                I only wish I could have said goodbye – it was so sudden, he was himself, two weeks ago he was mid-conversation and then he wasn't conscious – no wink, no squeeze of the hand, no –

She can't continue.

JOCASTA   We'll give the two of you a moment –

OEDIPUS   No, darling, you're / family too –

MEROPE   (*to* JOCASTA) Yes, do.

OEDIPUS   Mum, you have / to understand

MEROPE   I still need to talk to you, Oedipus, I didn't come all the way here for the celebrations, I need a few minutes of your time. I wanted to tell you before he –

                It's important.

MEROPE *looks like she wants* JOCASTA *to leave.*

JOCASTA   It's all right, I honestly don't mind / at all

OEDIPUS   I do mind. And however important it is, does it really absolutely need to be *tonight* –

I'm sorry.

,

God, my dad.

(*to* CREON) Well, I can't kill him now.

He's struck that this is an inappropriate thing to say –

If I am totally honest, if I am one hundred percent honest, I don't know if this feeling is relief or if –

JOCASTA   Sweetheart, your dad just died.

OEDIPUS   It puts things in perspective, the things that you were thinking, and then this – and they all just crumble away –

Are you sure that this can't wait?

MEROPE   Quite sure.

JOCASTA *makes to leave.*

JOCASTA   Well, your iron will certainly came from someone.

OEDIPUS   Sit down. You're my wife – and my mother, well, is going to need to learn to respect that fact. You two were inseparable at the beginning. I don't know what's happened – sit down.

Mother, can I get you a drink?

JOCASTA   I'll have one.

MEROPE *tenses up and then* –

MEROPE   I shouldn't. All right.

OEDIPUS *goes to find drinks.* CREON *exits. The room is now more or less empty.*

        Where is everything?

JOCASTA   Time's up on this place. Campaign's over.

MEROPE   And everything has to go tonight?

JOCASTA   Not our decision.

MEROPE   Are you looking forward to resuming your official role?

JOCASTA   No. Yes – it'll be a different thing, this time, as a mother. My memories are all of smoke in my eyes, hanging thick over the lamps.

LICHAS *enters and hands* OEDIPUS *a piece of paper, he glances at it, hands it back. The figures are getting more and more encouraging.*

OEDIPUS   We're going to make some history tonight, I think. Thanks.

LICHAS *goes.*

        The floor is yours.

MEROPE   Oedipus, I'm sorry to do this to you tonight – I don't know if we should have told you this years ago, or when you first spoke about your political ambitions, but then you made that announcement tonight, and I wanted to be with you tonight for the result, anyway – and, well, it's something your father felt very strongly about, but / he

OEDIPUS   Is this to do with the – the crossroads?

        When I was eighteen?

MEROPE   No, it's – why would it [be]? No. Oedipus, listen, we – that is, I –

I need you to put the whole 'birth certificate' issue to one side.

You need to leave it.

This is not in any way what OEDIPUS *was expecting.*

OEDIPUS   Why?

MEROPE   Because what happens next will be ugly, and you don't know enough to protect yourself.

,

OEDIPUS   Mum, with respect, I don't need political advice / and I understand [you're worried]

MEROPE   It isn't political. It's because it isn't real.

,

OEDIPUS   What do you mean it isn't real – my birth certificate isn't [real]?

MEROPE   No.

OEDIPUS   So, you've read something, or you've heard / something and

The pressure means that MEROPE *is sharp when she's interrupted* –

MEROPE   No. Oedipus. Please [listen].

We couldn't have children, your father and I. There weren't the options available in those days. We couldn't have them. And I thought about it and I asked your grandmother and I asked my friends, and being adopted myself, I did not want you to feel what I had felt, I wanted my child to have the thing I hadn't had. Which was silly.

OEDIPUS	Which is natural
JOCASTA	Are you saying / he's adopted
MEROPE	*Let me finish, girl, just LET ME FINISH MY SENTENCE.* This is about him, not about you. A wife is not, a / wife *is not…* / You *married* him: you aren't his flesh and blood.
OEDIPUS	Mum
	Mum

JOCASTA *stands up and leaves the room.*

MEROPE	Oedipus. Sit down. You're an only child because –

Oh God help me. We couldn't have them. We tried. I was so desperate for a family, for a baby, and it didn't *work*.

The reason you're an only child is we couldn't. We couldn't have them. And I loved your father, and so what do you do? Say goodbye? Start again as a new person, when you've already used up so much time. I was nearly thirty. I couldn't. But it was lonely. To accept: just us two, from now on, all the way to the finish line.

Until one afternoon your father's through the front door hours early, work clothes still on, speechless – and he takes me by the hand and we walk out of the house and he won't let me lock the door – and we're nearly running, it's a cold day, the light's going, and we're under the trees, you remember, and then suddenly he says, 'there' –

and lying naked on a strange bag, in a clearing a good way into the woods, we've come a good way, lying there, looking up at us, is a tiny, baby. Not yet a month old. A cloth holding his feet tight together, he's – a little grubby but he's not crying. Clear green eyes, lazy little smile. Soft head on the hard ground. Can't be more than a week old.

A gift from God. You were our gift from God.

,

OEDIPUS And so you kept me? You didn't hand me in.

MEROPE No. We were terrified for years that someone would claim you. Every knock on the door. No one did. We thought you must have been a traveller's child, an abandoned / child –

OEDIPUS And – am I?

MEROPE I – don't know.

OEDIPUS I need a cigarette.

OEDIPUS leaves the room.

MEROPE alone.

JOCASTA comes back in.

JOCASTA Where is he?

OEDIPUS comes back with a lit cigarette.

OEDIPUS He's here.

,

OEDIPUS smokes. There's a long silence.

Perhaps JOCASTA gets up and opens a window.

How can you falsify a person's birth certificate?

MEROPE　　It's a piece of paper, Oedipus – it is a piece of paper.

,

OEDIPUS　　Yes.

,

You have been my mother for my entire life. What you are telling me is that you started in the role a week later than I'd thought. And for that, I forgive you. That's the only thing that's changed.

Enter LICHAS.

Now what can we get you?

MEROPE　　Some sleep.

OEDIPUS　　All right. Come –

OEDIPUS *hugs* MEROPE, *who is suddenly tearful. And then he takes* JOCASTA*'s hand, holds it. He puts* JOCASTA*'s hand in* MEROPE*'s.*

I'm going to need the two of you even more after tonight. And I do need the two of you. We'll talk more tomorrow.

MEROPE　　Wake me up for the result.

OEDIPUS　　It's all right.

MEROPE　　Wake me up for the result.

MEROPE *leaves, followed by* LICHAS. *Just* OEDIPUS *and* JOCASTA.

OEDIPUS　　Where are the kids?

JOCASTA I don't know –

Is this about to become public knowledge?

OEDIPUS Yes. I don't know.

God, they've emptied this place while we've been in here. It looks like it looked at the very beginning.

It doesn't make a difference. It doesn't make the slightest bit of difference. That woman has loved me, fed me, taught me to *read* – and

they had nothing, those two, that fucking – it took him six months before he'd let me pay for his treatment – the two of them had nothing and no desire to have anything other than family, and they –

JOCASTA I know

OEDIPUS She loved me more than the woman who bore me.

JOCASTA How long have we got [till the result]?

CORIN *enters.*

CORIN I'm sorry to interrupt, but we really do need to think about –

JOCASTA Yes. Thank you, Corin.

CORIN *goes.*

OEDIPUS There'll be a way forward. A way to tell the truth.

JOCASTA You were adopted?

OEDIPUS Found. Abandoned.

JOCASTA But – who are your parents?

OEDIPUS	I don't know. She doesn't know. I don't know who I am.
	I'm not going to give that speech until I know who the man giving it is. I want to be able to stand before them and tell the truth.
	And I will.
JOCASTA	You don't need to go any further with this tonight. I am begging you. I am begging you to leave this and stop. It has been an unusual night, we've spoken about / difficult things
OEDIPUS	They could still be alive. My parents. My parents could still be alive. You of all people must – why would a woman deliberately abandon a child?
JOCASTA	*Please* just leave this, just for tonight – try and *be present*, live in what you've achieved, nothing has changed there – there's – what? A handful of seconds left now, before you're told / you've won
OEDIPUS	I have to find out who I am.
JOCASTA	Not right now you don't
OEDIPUS	I have to know –
JOCASTA	You know – you *know* who you are. I know who you are. It doesn't make a difference – it's two names on a piece of paper – these people handed you over as soon as you were *born*. You know the people who love you – and who you love
OEDIPUS	What's wrong with you? Worried you married into worthless stock?
JOCASTA	No – Oedipus, I'm asking you to / stop

OEDIPUS	Well, look, it won't be *you* – even if I was born to slaves born to slaves born to slaves, it still won't be on *you*.
JOCASTA	Please. Stop.
OEDIPUS	– but I am going to *know*. I won't stop until I know. I have to be more than a nameless baby lying naked in the middle of a wood –
JOCASTA	A wood?
OEDIPUS	The forest, the wild forest. Near my parents' cottage
JOCASTA	*That's* where they found you?
OEDIPUS	Yes – why does this / *matter*
JOCASTA	Shut up – stop – stop stop stop – just wait one second – ONE SECOND

,

She looks at him. She might almost be sick.

> You haven't seen it yet, have you? It *all* adds up.
>
> Oh God help me, it all adds up.

OEDIPUS   What all adds up?

To say this is to cross a boundary, and she knows that.

JOCASTA   after – after the birth, they took the baby, my baby I mean, and Corin was the last one to leave, he was a young man then, but Laius trusted him, I knew he'd be the one to have to [be responsible] and I knew how he looked at me, and I *begged* him, I said – *anything* rather than – just give the child a *chance* – but I beg you, don't let them murder it – let *nature* choose, I knew he wouldn't let my baby die –

                leave it in the woods, I said

            ,

    JOCASTA *looks at* OEDIPUS *as if for the first time. He looks up, back at her.*

    There is a long pause. The live countdown clock finally hits 00:00:00.

            ,

POLYNEICES   (*off*) MUM? DAD? DAD – DAD – DAD

    POLYNEICES *finds his parents.*

            HE'S HERE!

    ANTIGONE, ETEOCLES *and* POLYNEICES *come hurtling into the room, highly excited.* CREON *isn't far behind.* ANTIGONE *is taking charge of this.*

ANTIGONE   Okay, wait – I want before and after –

    ANTIGONE *takes a photograph of* OEDIPUS *and* JOCASTA.

            all on three

            one – two – three

E/P/A   YOU'VE WON YOU'VE WON YOU'VE WON YOU'VE WON

    The kids jump onto OEDIPUS *and he roars –*

    he screams from the very depths of himself –

    he throws them to the floor

    everyone is totally stunned.

            ,

JOCASTA   go. *just go*

CREON *and the kids leave – as they race along corridors, there's a lot of checking clothes, hair, and things.*

OEDIPUS *and* JOCASTA *slowly, automatically, change.*

OEDIPUS I'm thinking hard to find a way in which we might be wrong.

JOCASTA And can you?

,

OEDIPUS *is feeling in his pockets –*

What have you lost?

CORIN *enters.*

OEDIPUS The tie. I put it in there, safe, and they've taken it out –

CORIN It'll be through in the back – they've stacked everything in there until / it can be –

OEDIPUS I'll go, don't worry –

He goes to get it.

CORIN *has found* JOCASTA*'s glasses.*

CORIN End of an era.

JOCASTA I'm sorry?

Yes. For you as well, Corin.

I think sometimes you think I haven't noticed, or that – I don't know, that we don't realise, what you've –

CORIN *kisses* JOCASTA *on the back of the neck. It's one of the biggest moments of his whole life.*

,

OEDIPUS *comes back in with the tie, he hasn't overheard.*

CORIN I'll leave you two together for the final moments. Go well, Oedipus.

CORIN *goes.*

OEDIPUS *is putting on the tie, in the mirror.*

OEDIPUS It looks strange the other way [around]

He stops short. He puts his hands on the mirror.

It turns everything around but it stands still.

A mirror – turns everything around, but it –

He laughs. The third riddle is solved. But the thought is sad.

Did I only stand still?

,

I only wanted to know, to to move things forward, and to leave a mark

JOCASTA And you did. You do.

They look at each other.

OEDIPUS I'm sorry

JOCASTA For what?

OEDIPUS I feel I've – disappointed you, somehow

JOCASTA Oh no – oh no, no, I am *so proud* of you

Tonight. But every night before tonight too, every minute.

I want you to know in this moment that, through it all, *you* were loved. Not what you did.

> Not the mark you left. You. I love – you, for you –
>
> It was all you, always *you* –

OEDIPUS' *eyes might be full of tears.*

> You'll survive anything, I think –

They kiss and then they really, really kiss.

It's two people completely in love, and they know that they're saying goodbye. They roll onto each other, her heels kick off, they're reckless, they might have sex, they push each other's clothes up as if to take them off – and then JOCASTA *breaks it off – stands up – says, almost to herself –*

> I can't lose you twice

and she leaves the room –

and the stage, almost empty now, starts to feel like a dream.

OEDIPUS Mum?

MEROPE, *in her outdoor coat again. Just like the start.*

MEROPE I've heard the news.

OEDIPUS I didn't wake you up –

MEROPE There were other things [happening]

It's been quite the night

OEDIPUS Mum, I'm frightened –

MEROPE It was a struggle to get here.

A struggle to be here.

What can it be but a struggle to leave –

and step out to begin something new

MEROPE *leaves and then there's a bang, so loud it makes our teeth hurt. We see* JOCASTA *in another room. She's shot herself, lies motionless. Blood runs from* JOCASTA*'s wound. She's dead.* OEDIPUS *sees this.*

OEDIPUS *picks up something sharp –* JOCASTA*'s heel – he is oddly calm, now.*

The noise of the crowds, OED-I-PUS, stamp-stamp-stamp, louder and louder.

OEDIPUS *pulls down the skin below his eye, and precisely positions the point of the heel at the eyeball. With his other hand, he prepares to hit it hard –*

The crowd stamp and cheer and stamp –

and the curtain from the beginning suddenly falls and we are plunged into total darkness, surrounded by the noise of the crowds, ecstatic, deafening, relentless, for ten or twelve seconds –

and then, the curtain rises on a new scene, the same space –

but completely empty. Sparkling, white, new. It's two years earlier.

OEDIPUS *and* JOCASTA *are there, in different clothes, coats on. They seem happy. She has a beautiful orange scarf tied across her eyes as a blindfold. She's being led in through a door by* OEDIPUS *– he's saying 'step backward, step backward, here, stand here' –*

OEDIPUS   And turn around and – three, two

He takes the blindfold off. JOCASTA *takes in the space.*

This is it.

I wanted you to be the first to see it. It's a lease, wouldn't be permanent, and there's a process we have to go through, but I wanted you to / sign off before –

JOCASTA *puts her hand over* OEDIPUS*' mouth.*

JOCASTA   Stop talking, Oedipus.

She walks out into the space. Spins around.

,

I love it.

OEDIPUS   Yeah?

JOCASTA   Yeah.

This is the place. I love it. Already.

It feels like home.

As OEDIPUS *runs to* JOCASTA, *before he gets to her –*

The play ends.

TO KNOW THE SELF
Professor Simon Goldhill

Oedipus haunts modernity. It is a story we can't stop telling. For modernity, the figure of Oedipus has become an icon not just of Greek tragedy but of what it is to be a human.

Sigmund Freud's Oedipus marks a turning point in how modern Western culture understands itself. The Oedipus Complex is part of our language of self-understanding, whether we have read Freud or not, whether we agree with Freudian theories or not. Freud insists that Oedipus is part of who we are: he called every man Oedipus and Oedipus every man: 'Oedipus' fate moves us only because it might have been our own,' he writes. For Freud, Oedipus is a paradigm of what it is to be a human because the desire to marry one's mother and to kill one's father is integral, he insists, to the process of growing up, to becoming a sexual being. Freud had read Sophocles at school and travelled to see his generation's great performances of the play across Europe. He hoped to give authority to his foundational theory of sexuality by naming it after this classic of classics. When his friends gave him a medal to celebrate his career on his fiftieth birthday, it was inevitable that it would have an image of Oedipus on it and a quotation in Greek from Sophocles. They knew how much Freud was tied to the story of Oedipus. Our modern ideas of desire, sexuality, growing up, gender are inevitably informed by how Freud encountered Oedipus.

Yet there is a paradox at the heart of Freud's Sophocles. Oedipus himself is the worst example of the Oedipus Complex there could be. Oedipus actually does kill his father and have sex with his mother. His fate is very much *not* what every man experiences. He is horrified by what he has done, and blinds himself in response – and will spend years wandering as a beggar in self-hating misery and a social outcast. When Freud writes that Oedipus' fate 'might have been our own', his '*might have been*' veils the real difference between unconscious desires and horrific transgression. Oedipus fascinated Freud because he could see the 'might have been'.

Oedipus is an example of how terrible it would be if unconscious desires were enacted. Oedipus is terrifying, Freud argues, because he shows us things we cannot and must not know about ourselves. Freud, who constantly showed people things they could not and did not want to know about themselves, certainly could see himself in Oedipus. Oedipus was a story he couldn't stop telling himself, and us, about himself and about us.

Freud was not the only great thinker of modernity to be riveted by the story of Oedipus. From Hegel onwards, philosophers turned obsessively to Oedipus not just because Oedipus was a great portal to thinking about tragedy – why people had to suffer and how they should respond to the blows of life – but also because Oedipus was a figure who embodied the enquiring mind. Oedipus was the only person who could answer the monster's riddle of what has four feet in the morning, two feet at noon and three feet in the evening. The riddle's answer was 'the human'. For philosophers – and other writers and painters too – Oedipus was fascinating because of his search to know, *and* because the first and foremost answer was… the human – us. *Oedipus* asks us to know ourselves.

Sophocles' Oedipus – and the Oedipus of Robert Icke's marvellous retelling of *Oedipus* – is indeed a figure who prides himself on knowing and on seeking out the right answers. Oedipus promises the people that he will find the killers of Laius, the former ruler, although his death happened many years earlier. He insists he will search out the truth of his own birth. He makes these commitments despite the fact that people who care about him beg him not to go on with his relentless searching. In Robert Icke's *Oedipus*, Creon is shocked that Oedipus has made his promise to open an inquiry into Laius' death in public, without checking with his political advisers and publicity team. Creon, maven of modern political control of messaging, sees this as a rash piece of bravado. Oedipus' mother, Merope, repeatedly tries to stop him searching out and publishing his birth certificate, because she knows what uncertainty it will unleash. Jocasta desperately wants him not to look further into his birth, because she has worked out their true connection before he has. In each case, Oedipus pushes on towards what he wants to know. As the answer to the Sphinx's riddle is 'the human', so what Oedipus finds at the end of his quests is *himself*. An answer he does not want.

What has attracted so many writers towards the story of Oedipus is not so much the horror of his killing his father and having sex with his mother, acts committed in ignorance, but the way in which Oedipus' passion for seeking out the truth causes the awful reality of his life to become known. Like all of us, Oedipus *wants to know*, and is charismatic for the verve and authority with which he exercises his power in the search of the truth. Yet his tragedy – and Sophocles and Icke would agree it is our tragedy too – is that when you start to uncover the truth of how things are, it is likely to be *ravaging*. Oedipus blinds himself because he cannot bear to see what he now knows. The drama of *Oedipus* asks how self-destructive the human pursuit of knowledge will turn out to be.

Sophocles made knowledge sound out in the very name of Oedipus. The most familiar etymology of Oedipus' name is 'swollen foot', from the verb *oidan*, 'to swell', and the noun *pous*, 'foot'. His violent treatment as a baby has scarred his feet for life. His name indicates his condition, his inherited suffering, a sign of the past he cannot lose. Oedipus is reminded of why he bears his name in the play. But Sophocles lets another understanding reverberate in the theatre. The Greek verb, 'I know' is *oida* and the word for 'where' is *pou*. Through a series of puns, Sophocles turns Oedipus' name – *Oidipous* – into a question, 'Do you know where you are?' *or* an assertion, 'I know where I am.'

The tension between this question and this assertion constitutes Oedipus' condition as an adult. He always thinks he knows where he is, but he has not really learned where he stands or where he is going. In Sophocles' play, Oedipus thinks he knows that he was born in Corinth and left Corinth and came to Thebes as a foreigner. But he was, in reality, born in Thebes and is living all too embedded in his actual family home. When he comes to the place where three roads meet, he thinks he knows where he is going, but each of the decisions that he makes there about which route to take leads to tragedy. The swiftness with which Oedipus turns on Creon and accuses him of plotting against Oedipus' rule is a brilliantly dramatised display of Oedipus' misplaced certainty – with terrible consequences. There is real danger in acting on what you think you know... The story of Oedipus keeps getting told because it keeps reminding us of our dangerous arrogance. We want to know; we recognise knowledge is power. But there is real threat when you stand at the crossroads of your life. Do you think you know where you are and where you are going? The very word 'Oedipus' was used by Sophocles to remind his audience that confidence will lead to a tragedy of unintended consequences. *Oedipus* turns *knowing* into an urgent *question*.

Icke's transformation of Sophocles exists because Oedipus is a story that needs to be retold, still, and still again. The story of Oedipus is – as it always should be – absolutely modern. I do not mean that facile parallels between Sophocles' play and modern politics can be drawn. What makes the play compellingly of our time is not that Emmanuel Macron, the president of France, is married to a woman old enough to be his mother, nor that Donald Trump ludicrously tried to make Barack Obama's birth certificate a political challenge, nor that the murder of Laius in his chariot has become a joy-riding automobile accident. This production is compellingly modern because it goes to the heart of the ancient play.

The structure of Icke's staging is run through with two fascinating, interlocked dynamics. The first concerns the technology of knowledge and the relation of power in the public sphere. In Sophocles' play, Oedipus speaks like an orator in Athens to the assembled citizens of the city, sends to the oracle at Delphi for privileged knowledge, cross-examines the witnesses to Laius' murder like a forensic lawyer, takes control of the action. In Icke's restaging of Sophocles, Oedipus self-stages with flair in the media, receives statistical updates from his staff, runs his campaign for election with a practised mix of caution and confidence, encounters a threatening guru, and has the recognisable paranoia of those who have great but precarious power. Oedipus is elected because of his promises to use his knowledge to solve the problems of the state. What today's Oedipus shares with both a fifth-century BCE Oedipus and a nineteenth-century Oedipus – those other modernities – is a context when technology and elite knowledge are promising progressive solutions and transformative potentiality for society: science will cure, economics will make possible, regulation will order… And politicians rehearse their rhetoric based on such promises, and wield this assertive knowledge instrumentally. We need to retell Oedipus' story because the self-confidence of technology and political authority seems never to remember adequately the shadows of unintended consequences – nor to recognise how many of today's most frightening problems have been created by the unleashing of new knowledge, novel technologies. *Oedipus* asks us to struggle harder with the tragic potential of knowing.

The second trajectory is the family dynamics. Oedipus is shown in Icke's production not just in relation to Jocasta and Creon, but also to Antigone, and her brothers, Eteocles and Polyneices. For those that know Sophocles' other plays, the future both of Antigone's deathly clash with Creon, and of the fight to the death of the brothers, veins these scenes with ironies galore. But the story of Oedipus always asks how a family history intertwines with the history of the state. The richness of the portrayal of this family, including the fascinated discomfort we feel when we watch the eroticism between Jocasta and Oedipus, emphasises the deep emotions that are so often misrecognised in a politics based on technological solutions. *Oedipus* also asks what we need to know about ourselves, our motivations, our emotions, our desires, in the pursuit of political power – or what we need to unknow.

One of most brilliant moments of retelling is the close of Icke's play. When the final scene takes us back to a time before the disaster which has just unfurled before our eyes, Icke dramatises the tragic longing of what 'might have been'. As we see the happy couple start the political campaign in an empty room, we are faced with the questions of where did the tragedy start, where did it come from, how could it have been different. And to recognise that we do not know the answers to these troubling questions, for Oedipus or, most upsettingly, for ourselves. And here we are back at a beginning again. Waiting to tell the story of Oedipus once more. As we need to…

www.nickhernbooks.co.uk

@nickhernbooks